£2-00

To

7.

Vignette & Richard.

Nathan
ASTLE

Nathan ASTLE

With Phil Gifford

Hodder Moa

National Library of New Zealand Cataloguing-in-Publication Data

Astle, Nathan, 1971-
Nathan Astle / Nathan Astle with Phil Gifford.
ISBN 978-1-86971-096-5
1. Astle, Nathan,1971- 2. Cricket—New Zealand.
3. Cricket players—New Zealand—Biography.
I. Gifford, Phil. II. Title.
796.358092 dc—22

A Hodder Moa Book
Published in 2007 by Hachette Livre NZ Ltd
4 Whetu Place, Mairangi Bay
Auckland, New Zealand

Designed and produced by Hachette Livre NZ Ltd
Printed by Tien Wah Press Ltd, Singapore

Front and back cover: Photosport

This book is for Kelly, Liam, Alyssa, Mum, Dad, Lisa and Daniel.

Contents

Thanks

I'd like to thank every person who has helped me along the way —
I hope you felt your time, effort and kindness were worthwhile.

About the Author

Phil Gifford is the only person to twice win the New Zealand Sports Journalist of the Year award. He currently hosts the rugby show 'Front Row' on Radio Sport every Saturday, writes a weekly column in the *Sunday Star-Times*, is a regular on Sky television's 'The Press Box', and airs sports comments on Radio Hauraki's breakfast show.

The author of nine best-selling rugby books, and the creator of satirical rugby character 'Loosehead Len', he has hosted No. 1 breakfast radio shows in Christchurch and Auckland. He lives in Stillwater with his wife Jan.

Foreword

I must confess, on hearing that Nathan Astle was writing a book, I was somewhat surprised. To believe that Nathan was going to open up and give the reader an insight into what makes him tick was almost unbelievable. To get him to speak during a team meeting was like drawing blood from a stone, or more aptly, drawing a fiver out of his wallet. But now, as I put pen to paper, I am delighted that Nath has decided to share his life story.

I am honoured to be writing this foreword and feel privileged to be in a position to have spent so much time with him, professionally and socially.

Nath is a blue-collar, no-nonsense, get-the-job-done type of guy; well, that's what he would like you to believe. But underneath that perfect hairdo there is a delightfully complex character.

It's without question that he leaves the game as one of New Zealand's greatest-ever cricketers. He was athletic in the field, accurate and cunning with the ball, and wonderfully destructive with willow in hand. He was an entertainer. But it runs deeper than that: he was, and is, incredibly popular amongst his peers and players; young and old would always gravitate towards his company. He is fiercely loyal and although he hardly ever showed it publicly, he was incredibly passionate about playing for the Black Caps.

I found it very difficult to watch Nath have his position in the team put under pressure during the summer of 2006. It was obviously a difficult time for him, and I have no doubt it shortened his playing career. I will read that chapter with interest as, even though we are the best of mates, he never let on how deep it cut.

Knowing Nath as well as I do, he will be feeling very uncomfortable about the release of this book — he will be worried about what the boys will think and maybe a touch nervous about any contentious issues.

Relax mate, you're a great bloke and you have earned the right. You gave a lot and can give a lot more; your beautiful family will reap the benefit of that. Good luck with the book buddy, I hope it outsells *Cricketing Safari*!

Flem (Stephen Fleming), June 2007

Prologue: The Natural

The phrase 'he's a natural' is overused in sport by coaches, team-mates, and journalists like myself. Yet if anyone merits the label it's surely Nathan Astle, a cricketer who is almost a walking contradiction: very happy to drift away from the centre of attention off the pitch, but likely to bat in such a daring, dramatic way that even fellow players can be riveted by what they're seeing. On the day that he smashed an English test attack for 222 runs in Christchurch he brought most of club cricket in the city to a halt. Players wanted to adjourn to the clubhouse to watch his innings on television.

Astle had that kind of ability right from the start. His school coach, Steve Garland, reckons that the way he played for the Black Caps was little different from the way he played at Shirley Boys' High School. As a teenager, Astle didn't so much master opposing bowling attacks, says Garland, as smash them to pieces. And as you talk with the coaches he's been involved with in his life, it becomes clear that what's most remarkable is that once his father John had sorted out his most basic strokes, the rest of Astle's game was largely self-invented.

A recurring theme as I talked with Nicki Turner, the former New Zealand women's player who ran school holiday camps when Nathan was a boy, or Steve Garland, or the men who coached the Black Caps, was that Astle had his own way of batting, and, if he sometimes wavered when his form slumped, would ultimately come back to what had always worked best for him.

It's difficult to analyse the components in the performance of people whose gifts seem to be largely intuitive. John Kirwan's amazing 80-metre run for a try in the first game of the 1987 Rugby World Cup happened in a space that he has never been able to fully remember. He simply can't tell you how he did it: 'All I know is that when I got to the other end, I was really, really tired.'

But there are many clues along the way that help us understand more about the glittering cricket career of Nathan Astle; a career that includes 16 one-day international centuries and 11 test centuries, as well as 99 wickets in one-day internationals and 51 wickets in tests.

Nathan's hand-eye co-ordination is one of the first things mentioned by everyone associated with his cricket. Nicki Turner is sure that all the hours playing with a ball at the Astle home — a time that John made fun for his kids, never a chore — helped sharpen the skills.

And research that has examined the effect that play at an early age has on sporting development has led to some interesting insights into what underpins sporting talent. In the United States, a somewhat controversial scientist called Jonathan Niednagel, now a consultant to several professional sports teams, including the Boston Celtics basketball club, has been working for 30 years to determine what sorts of brains are best suited to various sports. By the end of the 1970s he'd begun to witness a correlation between certain personality traits in people and specific physical skills.

'The renowned Swiss psychiatrist Carl Jung had originally

identified personality characteristics such as extraversion and introversion, but he made no connection between them and motor skills. Simply stated, I found that certain "types" of people sharing similar mental characteristics with others *also* shared similar physical and even spatial abilities. Initially, it seemed far too improbable and unorthodox for such a connection, but I sceptically continued my research, part of which was coaching more than 50 youth teams over a decade.

'What this effort revealed to me was that each child (and adult) must be born with some sort of individual and specific genetic bent — actually regulating both mental and motor skills — and that these designs were limited in number. This empirical pattern (that is, a pattern based on observation and reality, not on theory) also demonstrated that certain groups of people shared similar inborn mental and physical aspects with others, independent of race, religion or ethnicity. In other words, people in different parts of the neighbourhood, city, or even the world for that matter, could share the same genetic design regulating specific mental and motor skills.'

Niednagel cites Larry Bird, Boston's hall of fame basketballer, as a prime example of what he calls the BEIR brain type. He writes that in the BEIR acronym, '"B" represents a genetic predisposition for the Back of the brain where deep concentration and intensity reside, as opposed to the front's active and energetic state, which minimizes contemplation.' (What could be a better prescription for a batsman than a brain that can concentrate for long periods of time, and apply intense concentration when a leather ball is unleashed from 20 metres away at up to 150 km/h.)

'"E" stands for Empirical,' says Niednagel, 'relying on sight and observation, instead of concepts and theory.' (This is similar to the way in which Nathan firmly believes that batting boils down to six words: see the ball, hit the ball.)

'"I" signifies the Inanimate world which is more interested in logic, systems, and things, than relating to people, pursuing harmony or trusting feelings.' (Never having been on a psychologist's couch, it's harder for Nathan, or those close to him, to draw any conclusion here, and it's probably drawing a very long bow to suggest that his neatness, which friend Geoff Allott describes as 'bordering on an obsession', qualifies as a great interest in logic and systems.)

However, consider the last letter, 'R', in Niednagel's acronym BEIR. 'It equates', he says, 'to the Right brain, the hemisphere adept at peripheral vision and smooth, adaptable motor movements, in contrast to the left hemisphere which specializes in tunnel vision and more mechanical, preplanned motor movements. Athletes born with the BEIR brain type can develop superior hand-eye co-ordination and athletic skills. This design is debatably the superior athlete in most sports. They also have the potential to develop consummate spatial logic.'

Spatial logic is the ability to calculate exactly where the body is in relation to its surroundings. In basketball, the prime example would be the way Michael Jordan could twist and move his body in mid-air on his way to the basket. For those who witnessed it, the catch Astle took on the boundary at Jade Stadium in 2006 to dismiss West Indian Dwayne Smith, leaping an extraordinary height to lodge the ball in his outstretched hand, would be as good a demonstration of spatial logic as you could find.

Niednegal even suggests what the typical BEIR-type person might be like away from sport, and the description fits Nathan like a glove. 'Though each person's upbringing and environment (past and current) influence his unique personality, the vast majority of BEIRs are more reserved and quiet due to their genetic imprint.'

So it is with Nathan, although it would be a complete mistake to confuse his quietness with shyness. We're talking about a man with a very keen sense of humour; one his best friend, Stephen Fleming, readily agrees borders on being wicked.

The first time I met Nathan Astle was in a radio studio in Christchurch in 2002, where Simon Barnett and I did the breakfast show. Nathan had been persuaded to come in on the Monday morning with Stephen Fleming to discuss his sensational 222 in the test with England the previous Saturday at Jade Stadium. Off air, Simon shook hands with Nathan, and, never having read about Nathan's unusual thumb (for full details see chapter 3), asked, as you would, if he'd been injured during the test. A flicker of a glance passed between Astle and Fleming.

'No,' said Nathan with a straight face. 'I was born like this. Most people are too polite to mention it.'

Fleming looked disgusted at the gaffe. Simon blushed to the roots of his suspiciously blond hair. And then, as he stuttered his apologies, Nathan and Stephen howled with laughter. So, I have to confess, did I.

They say to keep an eye on the quiet ones. When Nathan Astle had a cricket bat or ball in his hand it was a pleasure to take that advice.

Phil Gifford, Orewa, April 2007

222

Comedian Robin Williams once described cricket as being like 'baseball on valium', but he may have altered his assessment had he witnessed Nathan Astle's pyrotechnics on the last day of the test with England at Christchurch in 2002.

Richard Boock, *New Zealand Herald*

The day didn't start in any way that was remarkable. In fact, it shaped up as more likely to be a long, hard struggle, trying to avoid a loss. That day, 16 March 2002, a Saturday, began with a clear blue sky, a typical early autumn morning in Christchurch, but for those of us inside the Black Caps camp it was the wrong sort of weather. It was the fourth day of the first test against England and we were in trouble.

The equation was pretty simple. To win we had to score 550 runs in our second innings, which, if we managed it, would be a world record. By the end of the third day we had been 28 without loss, so the run-chase that we faced that Saturday was a mere 522. England had two full days to bowl us out. Any reasonable person would have thought that only rain could save us.

I usually sleep well before a game. On the morning of a game when you know you'll have to bat, you have a few nerves, and I always feel that way, but in general I have a handle on it. So, on that Saturday, it was business as usual and I had an early breakfast of toast and a cup of coffee — no different from what I'd usually have if I wasn't playing. When a game is played in your hometown you are given the option of where to stay — with the team or in your own home — and I'd stayed at home; so, after breakfast, I drove myself down to the ground. Later in the day, my wife Kelly was meeting her sister, who was getting married to Craig McMillan, to look at some possible venues for her wedding.

At Jade Stadium we had a team warm-up, and, after that, all I did with the bat was have a throw down session. I never have a net on the morning of the game. Half an hour before we started I went back into the shed, had a cup of coffee, and got ready. I was batting at No. 5, so I had the gear organised, but, as we started the day without a wicket down, I didn't have it on straight away.

Getting my batting gear on doesn't take long anyway. I wear very minimal protection. For me it's my box, my pads and a thigh pad. That's it. Some guys wear an inner thigh pad, but I never have. I've probably worn an arm guard a couple of times, but usually don't. For me, the less gear the better. I've tried little bits and pieces over the years in training but they've never felt comfortable and my movements have felt restricted. Although, it is fair to say that there have been numerous times I've wished that I had an inner thigh pad. I've lost count of the number of times I've been hit there off an inside edge, or when I've missed the ball completely.

I try to pretend that's a positive thing. I tell myself that I must be playing the wrong line, and being hit is just an eye-watering way of reminding me to get it right. Looking back on it, I probably should have worn an inner thigh pad a lot more. It's never pleasant at the time, but arguably worse is that the next day, when the bruise comes out, the guys in the shed find it highly amusing, and there are inevitably a few who take pleasure out of giving the bruise a bit of a poke.

In the first one-day game against Sri Lanka in Napier at the end of 2006, I was hit three times in the same spot by Chaminder Vaas. The bruise turned into a haematoma, and blew up like a balloon, so I had to miss the next game down in Queenstown. Luckily, that was the worst that ever happened.

Bruising wasn't an issue at Jade Stadium in the test with England, but surviving without a big loss was. We lost the first wicket of our second innings at the end of the sixth over of the day: Matthew Horne caught by their keeper James Foster off Andrew Caddick. Black Caps 42 for one.

Two overs later it became 53 for two. Lou Vincent, who had joined Mark Richardson, was caught at second slip by Mark Butcher off Caddick. Flem (Stephen Fleming) and Mark added a tough 66 runs together, but with just 15 minutes to lunch Caddick took his third wicket of the morning: Mark out, caught by Foster for 76, and New Zealand now 119 for three.

While I waited, a certain amount of anxiety built up, as it always did when I was waiting to bat in a big match. It was nothing untoward, and in fact I'd worry more if it didn't happen. I swear that I didn't go out there thinking, 'Let's belt it from ball one', because we were still in a bit of trouble, so my initial reaction was to try to survive for a while, and then see what developed.

We were three for not many, chasing 550. So I went out with a mind-set not a lot different from the attitude I'd taken into many other test matches. People have since asked me at what point I felt that I was seeing the ball so well that I could really go for it. But there wasn't any moment in the whole innings when I thought, 'From now on, I'm going to try to hit every ball for a four or a six'.

What developed over the 234 minutes of my innings just happened, and became undoubtedly the most bizarre day I've ever batted.

Stephen Fleming: The clean hitting, for such a long period of time, is the fond memory that I have.

I believe Nathan was at his best that day, and was simply enjoying the game for what it was. I would suggest that that was the most fun he ever had on a cricket field. He was hitting the ball and hitting with such a free spirit, that it epitomises what he would say about enjoying the game. If you asked him, I'm sure he would say it's the most fun he's had batting.

He just hit balls further and further. Everything he tried was ahead of the game. That's pretty unique for a player to have happen for so many runs. It's pushing to be the best innings I've ever seen while I was in the Black Caps. There would be other innings that have a bigger place in the heart because we won the game. But if you look at it for what it was, it would have to be No. 1.

Geoff Allott (Former Canterbury and Black Caps team-mate): What he created with that 222, among other things, was that he virtually stopped senior cricket in Christchurch. I was coaching at the time, and, literally, the game stopped.

We were playing East Shirley, his original club, and as he began blasting sixes all over the park at Jade, they were more interested in going into the clubhouse to watch the telly. That was the excitement he was capable of creating. Everyone knew that when Nath went out to bat, that although he wasn't a person who whipped up hype off the park, you knew something special could happen, despite the modest demeanour of the man.

There was a stage where I wouldn't say I was pre-empting where the bowler was putting the ball, but I just seemed to be in the right position, every single ball, to hit it pretty much where I wanted to hit it. I can't explain it. All I can say is that I was picking up everything bowled at me very early. When you're in form you see the ball, see what it's doing, as soon as it leaves a bowler's hand, and that's how it was for me that day. It meant I could get myself into a position to do virtually what I wanted with the ball.

When it's going well and your confidence is high everything is slower, and a lot clearer. You have time on your side and you tend to be focusing only on the ball. When you're not in form and are struggling, your anxiety is high, your breathing speeds up, everything speeds up, and you rush yourself, you worry about your feet, your backlift, where you end up, and in general you're not thinking about watching the ball, which is, obviously, crucial in a game of cricket.

Against the spinners and the medium pacers, when you're on song you can actually see the seam of the ball. With the quicker bowlers you see the seam later, and when you get a ball over 150 km/h, there's not much reaction time. You may still see the seam, but not as early or as clearly as with a slower bowler. I don't think people realise quite how quickly you have to react against someone like Shane Bond, Brett Lee or Shoaib Akhtar, those players that can regularly deliver a ball at over 150 km/h. That's pretty quick, and the bowler's only 22 yards (20.2 metres) away, so it arrives in a hurry.

On that day at Jade, the run rate didn't really start to take off until we were about six or seven down. My partners were going quite regularly at the other end. At 189, Flem was the fourth to go, out for 48 to a great ball from Andrew Flintoff that nicked through to the keeper.

I had a bit of a partnership with Macca (Craig McMillan) that went along at a reasonable clip, which is the kind of rate we both bat at normally anyway. We put on 53 together until Macca was out, caught and bowled by Caddick for 24, and we were 242 for five. Adam Parore was gone for one, deflecting a ball outside the off stump from Caddick onto his stumps, and Dan Vettori battled away before he went, the seventh wicket to fall, with the score on 300.

In the over before Dan went, I'd brought up a century with a four off Flintoff. It had come off 114 deliveries, so it was quick, but not exceptional.

Now we were into the tail-enders. Bowler Chris Drum went for one, lbw to Flintoff, and then, with Ian Butler joining me, and New Zealand eight down for 301, the pace started to pick up. England took the new ball, and 18 runs came off the first over: four fours and a two. But in the next over Ian was gone, caught by Foster off Caddick. We were 339 for nine.

Chris Cairns had suffered a patella tendon injury — one that would put him out for the rest of the test series — and if we'd been going really badly, he wouldn't have batted at all. But we decided to give it a crack, so Cairnsy came out with Lou Vincent as a runner.

I had no idea that the ground was filling up, no idea at all. It was one of those days when I was in my own little world, just playing cricket with the guy at the other end. It's hard to find the words to describe what happened out there. The best I can say is that for some reason, on that day, everything I'd trained and worked on in all my years of cricket came together perfectly. Why you can't do it every day, or even more often than not, I can't explain. But that day, for some reason or another, it all hit the middle of the bat.

I think it's the same in any sport — some days it's all pure; other days it's awful. And no matter how hard you try, when it's not working it never comes right.

What surprised me the most was how I managed to carry on striking the ball so cleanly for so long. Often in an innings, you'll go through a patch of 20 or 30 runs where you nick one here, nick one there, and you don't feel quite right. But not that day; for some reason or other it all hit the middle of the bat, sweetly and cleanly.

It's the fascination of cricket in some ways. It's like golf, you hit one really good ball in golf and it fires you up, and keeps on bringing you back. Similarly, in cricket you'll probably have more bad days than good, but those good days make you want to come back the next day and train harder.

David Trist (Former New Zealand coach): I did almost all of the last hour of Nathan's innings for radio.

It was just so decisive, so Nathan, and I was just so pleased for him. It was one of the most exciting times I've ever had, in anything. It just went on and on and on. It was a very special moment.

You might have seen things like that from a Viv Richards or an Ian Botham. But these characters were demonstrative; they were outgoing people, dramatic people. This was Nathan, a quiet man who wasn't out there in the media, in the limelight, telling stories, making little quips.

I think he played the way he played at Shirley Boys' High School, just a total demolition derby of anything and everything. I've talked since with a schoolmate of his who used to watch him when he was at school, and he said that Nathan used to just destroy teams. He didn't get 50 or 80 quietly, it was just total demolition, with balls going everywhere.

Perhaps that was the real Nathan. It came out a few times in his career, but not for as long, and not so much in a test match.

If he'd played like that all the time I guess selectors and coaches would have shied away, worried that they had a maverick on their hands, so they couldn't allow it, because this is cricket and here he was playing Twenty20 cricket 10 years before its time.

When I was with New Zealand, I always wanted Nathan to be himself. I recognised that he did have something that was very special. I was always sad when he got out, because he was always worth watching.

In the second over, Cairnsy and I had together hit 23 runs off Matthew Hoggard. I hit a six off the first ball of the over, Cairnsy hit one off the last ball. Then, in the next over, from Caddick, we took 20 runs. The live ball-by-ball commentary at Cricinfo was getting heated too:

(Over) 84.4: Caddick to Astle, SIX, AMAZING! Absolutely amazing cricket. Astle charges a good length ball outside off stump, gets a huge top edge over the slips and it sails all the way over the third man and that's also Astle's highest Test score, just like that.

(Over) 84.5: Caddick to Astle, SIX, UNBELIEVABLE! An incredible display of hitting from Astle, down the track to a full ball outside off stump, destroys it over extra cover, lands on the roof of the No. 2 stand and there's a long delay as they try to find the ball. That's 57 runs from 3.5 overs with the new ball, and this commentator professes to never having seen such destruction in any form of cricket match in person, this is breathtaking stuff. The ball is lost for good and they bring on a replacement.

When you're batting you do pick up the body language of the opposition, but to be honest the only time I really saw how much pressure Nasser was under was later when I saw the highlights on television. They went to his face a couple of times, and the way he looked, and some of the other guys who were fielding, gave me a good idea of the pressure they were under at the time.

> *Nasser Hussain*: I had been thinking that Astle and Danny Morrison had denied England a test victory on their last tour here, in Auckland, and could it happen again? Astle struck the ball brilliantly. We mixed it up but wherever we put it, he hit it for six. It was a magnificent test match. It was littered with great things throughout. Although the target was 550, I never took anything for granted, because cricket is a game that comes up and bites you.

And excitement levels for the commentators at Cricinfo weren't dropping either:

(Over) 86.1: Caddick to Astle, SIX, UNBELIEVABLE! Charges down the track, picks a ball on the up and smacks it hard and flat over extra cover, barely off the ground all the way, his sixth six.

(Over) 86.2: Caddick to Astle, SIX, UNBELIEVABLE! Astle is in sensational form, short rising ball, hooks this one over square leg, very flat but all the way, wide of the man posted just behind square.

(Over) 86.3: Caddick to Astle, SIX, UNBELIEVABLE! Speechless stuff! Down the track to a full ball outside off stump, sends it a country mile over long on, an almighty hit of biblical proportions.

Time for another replacement ball it seems, that one's out lost too, this new new ball lasts only 1.4 overs this time.

Hussain talks to the umpires, heaven knows what about, and drinks are taken. Twenty-five runs came off that over.

Gary Stead (Childhood friend, Black Cap, now New Zealand High Performance Centre coach): You think about Nathan batting, and you picture him charging down the wicket at Jade Stadium, hitting a bowler like Andy Caddick back over his head and out of the ground.

He could just make it look easy, and I guess the fact is he's worked hard to make it look easy.

By then we were 404 for nine, and I'd just got a double-century. When I got the 200 and it was the fastest 200 ever, I just ran down the wicket and raised my arms, and then just carried on batting, which is what I usually did when I'd got a century.

Lee Astle: (Nathan's mother) John and I were both at the ground. For the first time we got an invitation from New Zealand Cricket to go to lunch and see the game. It was absolutely brilliant. I cried my eyes out.

Kelly Astle: (Nathan's wife) I'd been looking at venues for my sister's wedding. Whenever we got into the car, we'd put the radio on, and they'd be saying how well Nathan was batting.

So I'd think, 'Should I go?'. But then there would be another venue to look at, so we'd carry on. It's terrible looking back on it, I laugh, but I'm embarrassed too. Can we leave this out? When it got close to the 200, I was going to go, and then it was too late. I just didn't make it.

It might sound odd, but to me it was just another day out there batting, and for some reason everything had clicked. I was playing my normal shots, and it just seemed that I could play every ball.

David Trist: At one stage I can remember saying, when Cairnsy was in, that if they could pull back the throttle, and bat sensibly, they could win the game. It couldn't lead to a fairytale ending going like this. Even though he scored 222, it was going to finish, it had to finish, and it did.

While I can't be absolutely sure exactly when Cairnsy and I talked, I think it was around that stage when we were over 400 that I said to Cairnsy, 'Mate, we can just pull back a little here, and try to pick up a few ones, they might pull the field in a bit, and then we can have another crack'.

He was going along alright too, and they had the field spread. Nasser Hussain just had no idea what to do in the situation. That was the one thing that sticks out in my mind. Thinking back on it, I believe we could have won that game if we'd maybe changed tack and just played normal cricket. Over the whole day, if I could go back and change anything, that's the one thing I'd love to go back to, so I could try a different tack. But Cairnsy said, 'No, just keep on going and we'll be finished by tea time'.

To this day, I joke that I blame him for us not winning the test. In the end we were only short by 98 runs.

So how will Nathan Astle be remembered?

The answer is simple. The long-standing veteran New Zealand batsman will, more than anything else, be remembered as the man who once made the sky above Jade Stadium rain with cricket balls, during one of the most astonishing batting onslaughts in the history of the game.

Most onlookers expected New Zealand's second innings chase for 550 to be all over before tea.

Instead, those who braved the unlikely situation to turn up for the start of play, and those who later streamed to the ground as news of Astle's phenomenal innings spread, were treated to a once-in-a-lifetime experience.

The dyed-in-the-wool Cantabrian has played many great hands during his career, as his 11 test centuries and 16 ODI tons can attest, and he leaves the game as one of New Zealand's most influential players, and arguably their best ever ODI batsman.

If pressed on his career highlights, his usual modus operandi is to move away from his personal achievements and concentrate on some of his favourite team moments — such as the 1999 test series win in England, and New Zealand's first victory at Lord's.

But nothing the 35-year-old has done before or since will ever dissuade me that his most compelling performance — and one of New Zealand cricket's most famous days — revolves around his 222 against England five years ago.

So dramatic was it, that, within hours of his breathtaking and record-destroying innings, his deeds had gate-crashed the Wisden 100 — the list from the cricket world's 'bible' ranking the great and heroic acts in the history of the game.

Though it was not enough for New Zealand to avoid defeat in the opening test, the manner in which Astle raged until the end ensured his effort would be remembered long after the result.

In a match that swayed from one spectacular individual performance to another, Astle struck the fastest double-century in history in terms of the number of balls bowled, raising his second hundred off a mere 39 deliveries.

Of the 11 sixes he smote, two sailed onto the roof of the No. 1 and No. 2 stands and left some of the most respected names in the game — Ian Botham, Bob Willis, Martin Crowe, Ian Smith — virtually babbling over his strike power.

Described by one English newspaper as the best hometown innings since Geoff Boycott made his 100th hundred at Headingley in 1977, Astle's contribution was a tad different in approach, to the extent that it even gave his side a faint chance of scoring the world-record 550 to win.

In terms of dramatic New Zealand losses, his near miss probably ranked alongside the courageous run-chase at Trent Bridge in 1973, and the emotion-charged scenes at Johannesburg in 1953 when the tourists were battered by Neil Adcock and devastated by news of the Tangiwai train disaster.

Astle's extraordinary innings, lasting just 168 deliveries and including 11 sixes, 28 fours and two lost balls, pushed him into the Wisden list at 71st place, though if New Zealand had won the match he would have apparently made the top 10.

His second century contained nine sixes — all of which would have delighted bat-makers Kookaburra with the distance they travelled, and hinted at the savagery brought to the game by the likes of Sir Vivian Richards, Ian Botham or Sanath Jayasuriya.

It was the sort of day that rendered the idea of one-day internationals almost nonsensical, when the familiar claim of test cricket being boring was shown up to be the fallacy it always was; and when one man's last stand stole the hearts of a nation.

The only people who weren't exactly dancing in the aisles were the ball suppliers for the Canterbury Cricket Association, a group of nervous used-car dealers in the adjacent street, and the disbelieving England pace bowlers.

A couple of distinct memories involve England swing bowler Matthew Hoggard, who laid waste to New Zealand's first innings batting with seven wickets, taking one for 142 off 24.3 overs in the second, and Andy Caddick conceding 25 off an over before being taken from the attack.

Apart from the bruised pride of the England bowlers, the other noticeable problem was the potential for serious neck injuries, as fieldsmen, bowlers and the crowd alike tried to keep their eyes on a series of disappearing objects.

The maelstrom prompted Wisden.com's assistant editor Lawrence Booth to suggest that, if former cricket writer Raymond Robertson-Glasgow was right about Bradman's batting being a mixture of poetry and murder then, for a brief hour, Astle was Shakespeare and Jack the Ripper rolled into one.

Richard Boock, *New Zealand Herald*, January 2007

When it was over, I was aware of what I'd done, but it was some time before I realised what the reaction was in the wider world of cricket. Walking back through the changing shed after having been dismissed was surreal. On a personal note, it had gone well and I could be happy with that, but my gut reaction was that we'd lost the game.

From outside I could hear the Barmy Army as they kept on chanting, reminding me that I'd dropped Graham Thorpe when he was on two, and that he'd gone on to make a hundred. They had a song, that went something like, 'You might have got the world's fastest hundred, but you dropped Thorpe'.

It wasn't until I sat down, saw the highlights, and watched it myself, that I realised it was a pretty special day, not just for me, but in world cricket. In the days after, I struggled to explain to the media what my feelings were, and to this day I still find it very hard to explain in more detail exactly how I felt at the time.

I've watched the recording of the innings, and it's clear that at the time I didn't show a lot of emotion. The only time I did was when one of the sixes I hit, a straight one, went over and out of the ground. I let a little bit of emotion out there, and yelled out 'Yeah!'. Cairnsy had been jibing me that my sixes weren't as big as his, and when that one went straight down the ground and out of the park, I thought it was a reasonable hit. I think between overs I went up to him and said something like, 'That wasn't too bad, was it, pal?'.

We had a few beers in the shed after the game, with the guys saying well done. I think there were a few, including me, surprised at what I'd done, but there was no celebration. We all knew that we'd lost the test — and within a day or two we had to travel to the next game.

I've never been one to collect a lot of memorabilia, but I have stored away the bat I used that day. I've got a helmet that Flem and I signed from the first game we played together for New Zealand, and a couple of stumps tucked away that I'd have to look up to see what they're from, but, in general, I've never been one to swap shirts or that sort of thing. We do get given a lot of gear, and I have kept one shirt from every series I've played in. I give the rest away, to charities, schools, and a little to my family. I'll end up with the cupboard pretty bare apart from the shirts.

I used the 222 bat only a couple more times, because it was starting to get cracked at the bottom. A gentleman called Baz Gibson in Christchurch, who has fixed my bats through the years, fixed that one for me and I got a few more runs through the series with it. Does it have a lot of red dots on it? No, it's pretty clean.

I put it away at the end of that series and it's now turned a dirty brown colour. I'll probably get it cased up and hang it somewhere one of these days. It's a good memory for me; one of the special days of my career.

Like a Duck to Water

As a kid, my life was almost totally dominated by sport. That may not surprise you, but when I look back, it does surprise me. You see, it wasn't as if I had pushy parents, the nightmare ones you read about — for example, in women's tennis — who want to live their lives through their kids' sport. The kind that force kids into training endlessly, so all the pleasure that should be gained from childhood sport is lost.

At our home, it wasn't even remotely like that. One of the great things about Mum and Dad, Lee and John, was that they never pushed me to play any particular sport; instead they gave me the options and let me do pretty much what I wanted.

They were never parents to stand on the sideline and yell and scream. Mum says that she used to watch kids' soccer and be acutely embarrassed at the behaviour of some of the parents on the sideline.

So one of the best memories I have of them when I was growing up was that they weren't aggressive, demanding parents about sport, the type administrators target as the ugly parents. In saying that, if I wanted to do something in sport — and as long as I can remember, I did want to play — then they were fully behind me and gave me every opportunity they could. Sport was always around, they just made sure that we played for fun, that it was our choice, and not because they wanted us to. My sister Lisa remembers that as kids we virtually never spent any time blobbing in front of television, there was always something active on the go.

As long as I can remember, when there was spare time I always wanted to kick a ball around or play cricket, a lot of it with my brother and sister. But my first involvement with cricket must have started earlier — earlier than I can remember — as there's a photo of me when I was about four, in the backyard with a bat in my hand, playing with Dad.

It was pretty much a family thing, not so much a neighbourhood affair. Sport was something we knew, and something we had fun with. Nothing else really interested me.

We were a very close family, which is something you become more aware of when you're older, the fact that you did so many things together, which gives you so many good shared memories.

Lee Astle: When the kids were growing up we had a rule that anyone could call a family forum if there was something annoying them. You aired it at the table, and you couldn't leave until it was settled.

We've stayed close, too. It helps that we all still live in Christchurch, so we see each other reasonably often — although Lisa has moved all the way out to Darfield (45 km west of Christchurch), which we all suggested to her is a long, long way out of town. Occasionally, she complains that she's out of the family loop now, but that's not really the case.

But as far as my family goes, and staying together, I have to admit that there were times when I was slack while I was playing internationally, especially when you look at all the support I was given. You go away for a long time, and when you come home, even though it's your family and they haven't seen you for a long while, you often feel like just being at your own home, quietly, by yourself.

At times, when I've come home and not made the effort to catch up as often as I should have, I've been aware that I was being a bit selfish. Our family are all born-and-bred Cantabrians. I'm the eldest, then there's my sister, Lisa, who is 20 months younger than me, and my brother Daniel, who Mum tells me was born three years and five months after I was born, to the day.

We lived in Shirley when I was growing up, and I didn't leave the area until I moved from home to a house that Stephen Fleming and I bought in Beckenham when we were starting to be paid to play cricket. My parents both worked. My mother is a hairdresser still, and Dad is an interior decorator, which meant that he worked from contract to contract, which allowed him to arrange his work around our sport when it suited.

They were both keen supporters, but Dad was probably the one who ran us around the most. Mum did when she could, but because of her work commitments, it was mostly Dad at the wheel and at the grounds. Both played sport. Dad played club cricket and a bit of rugby; Mum, netball and softball; and they were both good at table tennis.

John Astle: There was no great family history in sport, but Lee and I both enjoyed playing, and we were happy to spend time with the kids playing different games.

Lee Astle: John was very patient with them when they were trying to play when they were small. More patient than I was.

John: I remember starting them at table tennis, putting

a box at their end of the table so they could get up high enough to play. I suppose that probably helped them a bit later on, playing with a bat and ball at a young age.

Table tennis was a sport that Daniel played to a high level, representing New Zealand in age group teams. It's also the only sport in which four of us played in the same team. Dad, Lisa, Daniel and I played together for the Avonside club in 1987, and we won the Canterbury club title for our grade. We were all at about the same level in table tennis for a while, then Lisa and Daniel carried on after I flagged it, and they kicked away from me.

There was nothing very dramatic about my pre-school days, but there was something unusual when I was born, on 15 September 1971, in Christchurch. I arrived with two thumbs on my right hand. The thumb I still have only moves from the base, pretty much at right angles. The other one came back out like a pair of clippers.

They had to decide which one I would keep when I was very young, and the one next to my index finger was removed. I was only a baby, so I have no memory of it at all.

One consequence of this is that when I hold a cricket bat my right thumb wraps around the handle very easily. The only difficulty I've ever had with it is that occasionally I get a pair of gloves where I can't get my thumb into the right one, but it's never stopped me doing anything. They tell me that they could break the bone in the middle and reset it to make it less noticeable, but I would still only be able to move it from the base and still wouldn't have any power in it.

Every now and then I'll look at it, and go, 'What the hell is that?', but it's never bothered me, never stopped me doing anything. In fact, as I play pool left-handed, it's a handy cue-holder. At school I went through a stage where I was being teased a bit — 'Tom

Thumb', 'Crooked Thumb', that kind of thing — and I went to Mum and Dad and asked if they could get an operation to have it straightened. They persuaded me that I was probably better off the way it was, and I got through the phase okay. It's unique to me now, I think. Even now, when I shake someone's hand they start a bit. It's even become a bit of a party trick.

Sport has always been my love and passion. As a small boy I was playing club soccer and cricket, and to be honest it was what I was most interested in at school.

My sister Lisa, who played in the New Zealand women's cricket team in 1993, spent a lot of time playing cricket in the backyard, or going down with me to the nets at a park or school. We had our disagreements, and while there were the normal sibling scraps, most of the time Dad was either with us, or we shared the time batting and bowling happily enough. At that age, it doesn't strike you as anything unusual, your younger sister having cricketing talent, but looking back on it, she was pretty good from when she was quite small.

Lisa: Was he a generous-spirited big brother? Yes, he was. I don't remember being pushed aside when a ball and a bat was out. I really can't remember the boys ever teasing me, or saying they didn't want to play with me because I was a girl.

John: Lisa just grew up with the boys, with all of them batting, bowling, and catching. There were no special divisions over who did what. She liked to keep up with the boys.

Lee: It's very hard to imagine Lisa being pushed around. She wasn't one of those sissy little girls who'd stand back, she was a pretty strong little thing. I have a memory of the three of them in a line, John with a bat, hitting the ball to them to catch. Were they competitive with each other? Not really, certainly not to the point where they'd fight over it.

All three of us, Daniel, Lisa, and I, were reasonably well co-ordinated with a bat and ball.

Daniel: I remember playing a tremendous amount of backyard cricket, but the biggest thing I remember about Nathan when we were kids was the day he decided he'd been a smart alec and throw darts at my feet to try to make me dance.

It didn't quite work out, because, as I remember it, all three stuck in my leg.

Nathan: My memory is that it was just one.

Lisa: A lot of the games we played did just involve the family. There weren't many other people there. We had enough to play cricket amongst ourselves.

Lee: So they'd be playing, I was the umpire, and over the fence was out.

Lisa: When I was about nine or ten, I played cricket in a team with the boys at school, which never seemed unusual to me. There weren't really any girls' teams I could play with.

John: There would be the occasional boy who would make smart comments about playing against a girl in those club sides. That usually stopped when Lisa bowled them out. (Laughs.)

Gary Stead: I can never remember going to the Astles and playing cricket. I can remember going there a lot, and having a wonderful time, playing table tennis or pool, and Lee would make us something to eat. Maybe you had to be an Astle to be invited to join in the cricket. (Laughs.)

Nathan's family have always been great people. Johnny, who had more free time than Lee, was a wonderful support for Nathan. He was there almost all the time, but never in an intrusive way, sort of standing quietly at the edge of a building while a game was going on, not making any fuss. But Nathan knew he was there, knew he was supporting him.

Both his parents are great people, very humble, and not the sort of people who would make a fuss out of the fact their children were doing so well in sport. But the fact that all three children were such high achievers at their chosen sports is really remarkable. It shows how extremely important healthy support is for a budding sportsperson.

In the coaching world we now talk a lot about the ugly-parent syndrome, having people too involved, and yelling out from the sideline. Not once did that ever happen with the Astles.

Stephen Fleming: Knowing Nathan, and Gary Stead, and the families, went back to primary school days. We'd play in primary school teams and the families would go to places all around the South Island, and camp a lot of the time.

Nathan's a bit older than me, but the families first got to know each other then. We'd all be parked up for a week or two and they'd share a bit of time on the sideline. Nath and I would be playing cricket, so it was quite early on when the connections were made.

Nicki Turner (Childhood coach, now head of the School of Sport at Auckland Unitec): One of the shames for children growing up now is that there's so little space around houses that kids can't spend time just playing, mucking around, pretending to be their heroes in the backyard, basically just spending time developing eye-hand skills.

The Astles spent a lot of time doing that, and John was almost unique in that there are a lot of parents who put pressure on their kids to get it right, pushing them to never miss a catch.

John and Lee were never like that; they were very, very supportive. They were part of quite a big group of parents around at the same time that Nathan was in the Under 14s, who were excellent in that respect. There was none of the unhealthy pressure that's put on a lot of kids.

There were mums, dads, and grandparents too, who were there at the games supporting, and John and Lee were terrific. They weren't living through their kids, they were there having fun, and enjoying the success of all the kids, not just their own. As a coach I've seen parents who have really made it difficult for their children, and are there for the wrong reasons. But that group was lovely to be around.

Denis Aberhart (Canterbury and New Zealand coach): His parents are great people. They're a very close-knit family, that have been really good supporters of the kids all the way through. If you see his mum and dad, you see Nathan. All the way through he's had total, no-strings-attached support from his whole family. That's why he's like he is.

You might wonder why, in a province like Canterbury where rugby is so big, I didn't give rugby a go. Well, I did, but it wasn't too successful. Dad took me down a couple of times to New Brighton rugby when I was very young, maybe six years old, but he says I wasn't really interested. Apparently, I was inclined to run away from, rather than towards, the ball.

I asked Dad quite recently why he didn't give me another go at rugby, and he laughed and said, 'You never asked to go back. And you know that if you'd asked, I would have taken you.' So after the very brief time with rugby, Dad gave me a crack at soccer, and that was something I enjoyed right from the start, and kept playing. My rugby days will always be limited to a six-year-old running away from the ball.

In all the age groups, I got into a few Canterbury cricket teams, but I was actually more successful in soccer. In my memory, I was in representative age group sides from the time I was about 12, right on through. It was a terrific time right throughout New Zealand to be a kid enjoying soccer. When I was 11, the All Whites went to the World Cup, and names like Steve Sumner, Grant Turner, Ricki Herbert and John Adshead were household names.

The one big memory I have about the sport at international level from when I was at school was the All Whites at the World Cup.

So while the cricket was going okay, at the time it wasn't quite the buzz that soccer was. I was what I guess you'd call a lazy footballer, playing midfield on the right, then up the front, anywhere that didn't require much running. I wasn't an Energiser Bunny on the soccer field.

Steve Garland (Shirley Boys' High School teacher and cricket coach): He was a very good soccer player, at a time when soccer in New Zealand was keen to have young players committing everything to soccer.

Stuart Thomas (First soccer XI team-mate): Nathan played either as a striker, or in the midfield, very much in an attacking role. He had a great ability to be in the right place at the right time, and he struck the ball really well. He had genuine talent, he was very fit, and he had plenty of heart. If there was someone going to do something to win the game for you, it was more than likely going to be Nathan.

Not everyone sticks in your memory from so long ago, but he does. Underlying everything was the feeling that in sport he could pretty much do everything. You felt that if he played badminton, he'd be a star at that as well. Whatever he wanted to do in sport, he'd pick it up and do well. And he was a good guy. There was no spitefulness in anything he did.

Gary Stead: Nathan was always solid and fit, and liked to look after himself. He basically had a good sporting body. But he was never a massive guy who got there on being bigger and developing earlier than other boys.

We played in the Canterbury primary school team together, and we played against each other in club cricket when we were about 12 years old. Nathan was in the first XI at Shirley Boys' in the third form, and he was playing against guys like Richard Petrie and Darrin Murray, who were seventh formers who would go on to represent New Zealand.

The thing was that he went in and succeeded immediately, which proved how much talent he had. I don't think he ever struggled with that level. I really think that whatever he wanted to do he would have been able to do it. Very naturally gifted with feet and hands.

I remember watching him play soccer, and I recall thinking, 'You can be a lazy bugger'. Sometimes he would just stand near the strike zone, and I'd think, 'Imagine how good you could be if you ran round a bit'.

In the seventh form, Nathan and myself both played senior cricket, which was very unusual in those days. That was a topic that stirred up a lot of debate. I'm inclined to think some schools hold kids back when there's no need to. If you look back, Nathan could have played senior cricket when he was 15.

At school he was a reasonably sharp bowler but it was

as a batsman that he was outstanding. I'd bat at No. 3 and he'd bat at No. 4, and our No. 5 at times wouldn't even pad up, because he knew Nath could be out there forever. He was pure class at school level. He would just hit the ball all over the ground. He had more power than the vast majority, hitting sixes with the strength of a man, which he developed earlier than most of us.

My main influence in soccer was probably Terry Conley (who took Christchurch United to four Chatham Cup victories and was technical director of New Zealand Soccer). He was a very good coach, and tremendous friend to me. I got into the Under 19 squad for New Zealand, but we didn't actually play a game. At that stage it had got to a point where soccer trips were starting to overlap with playing cricket, and I had to make a decision, and cricket was obviously the one I chose. By then, I think I could see more potential for the future in cricket.

Promising cricketer Nathan Astle has withdrawn from the national development soccer squad, which has been training over summer.

Coach Terry Conley says had Astle been available he would have gone close to selection for the New Zealand youth team for the world event in Papua New Guinea in September.

'He's made a choice, and good luck to him,' said Conley. 'Unfortunately nowadays you just can't play both at top level any more. They overlap so much.'

Christchurch Press, January 1988

When I think back, just about any sport I wanted to play came reasonably easily to me. I guess it was down to that hand-eye co-ordination. Cricket certainly came naturally to me. I've never really worked on technique; there are things I've refined, but from the time I was a kid it was always a case of 'see the ball, hit the ball', and that's the way I've tried to play most of my career.

I guess right from an early stage there could be those who thought I had a lazy approach to my sport, but I really feel that's more to do with my manner than the reality. I've always done what I thought was enough for me. I've never over-trained, never spent endless hours in the nets at one time. I've done what I think I need to do. I think if I were one to train for hours on end, I could have lost my enthusiasm for the game. Some might think that's wrong, but I believe you have to work out what's best for you. Some may say that if I had trained more, I could have been better, but I'd say that my career would have been a lot shorter if there had been hours of work in the nets.

There was never a coach, certainly not one that I can remember, that tried to change my technique — a word you won't hear used a lot about me, and certainly not with the adjective 'classical' before it. Dad was my coach for a number of years, and when I went into school and age group teams there were no drastic changes made to the way I played.

I got a grounding in the game at home from Dad, and I used to go down to parks in the weekend, and watch him play as well. As a kid you pick up basic things, and I'm sure that when I was very small he would have shown me how to hold the bat, the proper stance and so on.

When I was young, before I went to secondary school, many of us kids went to coaching programmes after school and in the holidays that were organised by David Trist and Murray Smith, from Canterbury Sports. Our main coach was Nicki Turner, who right through the 1980s played tests and one-day internationals for the New Zealand women's team.

John Astle: I showed him the basics of the game, things like a forward defensive shot. He used to pull the ball a lot, and there were times when he was criticised by coaches along the way for that, but I don't think they realised how many runs he scored with a pull shot.

Lee Astle: Nathan was told by John Howell [former director of batting at the national high performance academy] that he needed to change. I wasn't that happy about that, because my feeling was that if you had natural ability you should be able to stick with that.

John: Having said that, I don't know that there was a coach who really made a concerted effort to get Nathan to change his technique. In time he just found his own way really.

Nicki Turner: I was at university and David approached me to help out with the coaching. John and Lee booked Nathan, Lisa and Daniel in for the first courses we ran. So I had the three of them. I think Nathan was only about 10 and Lisa a year younger. Back then, if you'd put Nathan and Lisa side by side there was very little difference between them technically. They were very similar players.

Daniel was a bit younger and he was there for a couple of years before he went on to concentrate on table tennis, but Nathan and Lisa had quite a bit of coaching. In the school holidays we'd have about 90 minutes every day.

Did I ever try to change Nathan's style? I can remember saying to him, 'You're going to have to learn to drive off the back foot. You can't cut everything off the back foot.' (Laughs.) I'm so glad he didn't listen to me. He was one of the few players internationally who was able to cut the ball off the stumps, maybe even middle.

When you are coaching, you do come across a few young

people who have the ability to really know what's best for them, without coming across as being cocky or arrogant. You would never use those words to describe Nathan when he was young.

I had him in the Canterbury Under 14 and Under 16 sides, and he just had the ability to work out from what you were saying what bits of the message were right for him at that time.

As they got older, about 12 or 13, I would talk with a number of the youngsters about how they could develop an ability to talk with adults when they wanted to contribute to their game; to tell them things and give them advice. We talked about how to be respectful, and acknowledge that advice, but then be able to work out for themselves which bits they would use. We discussed the language they might use: thanking people; saying the advice was interesting; and that they would give it some thought.

A lot of kids who were getting earmarked as having some potential would have a club coach, a school coach, perhaps someone like me, and then maybe Granddad or Grandma or Mum or Dad, all giving lots of advice. Nathan was one of the few who didn't need to learn that from me, because he just had the ability to do that anyway. He had an understanding of what was going to suit his game.

We spent a lot of time in the holiday programmes working on technique. We weren't just having nets. We worked on all of the shots, all the bowling techniques, off cutters, leg cutters, all trying to equip them for when the summer came.

Nathan and Lisa had almost like a twin relationship when we were training. You know how twins will often, not compete, but try to assist each other. They were a lot like that.

They trained very well together. Because Lisa was a very skilled player herself there wasn't any question about, 'You're my sister, and you're younger, so I don't want you around', which you'd often get from young kids, especially if they're playing the same sport.

I think Nathan had an ability to recognise when people were good at what they were doing. And if you'd seen Lisa as a child, and then later, when she went through to play for New Zealand, they were very similar players. Real touch, instinctive players. They may not have been technically the best players when they were young, but they had that flow, a really good eye, and they had nous too.

Both had the ability to think through where they had to bowl at a particular person. Even then, it wasn't just their batting, they were both very useful bowlers. As youngsters they were quite slight, so both of them learned how to do things with the ball, because they couldn't rely just on power.

Nathan was just one of those kids who you knew was going to be something special in the sport. There are some people who just have that X factor. He always had the desire to succeed, but not in a way that some people have, where they're excessively competitive. It wasn't that. With Nathan I think it was that he genuinely loved what he was doing. It wasn't hard work, it wasn't even a burning desire to always win, it was just a deep-seated love of the game and wanting to do the best he could in it.

Lisa was exactly the same. I believe that Lisa could have been in New Zealand women's cricket the same as Nathan was for New Zealand men's cricket. I don't know exactly why Lisa didn't play for as long, but she was one of those unfortunate players where she had a long run of injuries at crucial times. You play so irregularly in women's cricket that if you miss a couple of tours your career is almost over.

If she'd been able to play more, people would have seen a person with just as much ability and just as much exceptional talent.

One innings that really sticks out for me from my childhood was my first hundred. Dad had bought me a Slazenger cricket bat from Anderson and Hill Sports, and it came with a promise that if you got a century with it, you got a package of free gear. I think I was about 13, and I can remember how much I enjoyed getting the hundred. I've been lucky enough to enjoy many hundreds in my career, but I still remember that one and the thrill of reaching the milestone.

Cricket was just something I could always do. Being able to bat and bowl never seemed remarkable or special to me. I just always felt comfortable when I was playing — and it's one of the things that later you'd like to be able to recapture, because when you're older it's easy to analyse too much, which can lead to stress, which can lead to less success.

As you get older, experience can muck you around a bit. You can lose that 'no fear' attitude. Playing as a school kid, I was never really nervous, it was much more a case of wanting to get out there and do something that brought me pleasure.

Steve Garland: We always knew who the good players were coming through from the Shirley cricket club.

At the first assembly I would have told all the boys who were interested in cricket that there would be trials after school in a few days. We would pick junior teams for games with Southland Boys' High early in the first term from third and fourth formers, and Nathan was in that side.

John was the perfect supporter, a hell of a pleasant guy,

who you could have a chat with on the sideline, who never used that time to suggest that his boy should be batting higher in the order, or opening the bowling.

Gary Stead: It wasn't just cricket, it was every sport Nathan took on. He was a soccer player, who could come along to rugby, which I played, and kick goals from halfway. He was also the king of the school table tennis table. Every lunchtime there were always people queuing up, trying to knock him off the top of the table.

He was extremely popular at school. People gravitated to him, but I don't know that he was extremely comfortable with that. As he got older he seemed to prefer to shun the limelight if he could. But whether he liked it or not, as a school kid he was a name that was on people's lips.

As a schoolboy I should have been as nervous as hell playing my first game of senior cricket, but going out to bat as a boy against men didn't feel like anything too daunting. I really don't believe it was arrogance, only the unspoiled confidence of youth. It just felt like a natural thing to do.

The only uneasy time with the bat as a schoolboy was not in senior club play, but in a school tournament when young Christopher Cairns was playing. He was about the same size then, as a 14- or 15-year-old, as he was when he played for the Black Caps, so he was a hell of a lot bigger than the rest of us. I can remember facing him at Ilam Park, and I'm pretty sure I was a bit scared about facing this boy-giant.

Gary Stead: As a youngster, Nathan had outstanding skills, and people in our age group all talked about him, from when he was about 13 up until 18. There was actually a fear factor about him at high school, bowling as well as batting. He often bowled pretty aggressively, and would toss in the odd bouncer. He had some angry blood in him. (Laughs.) In one club game he knocked an opposing batsman's four front teeth out. It was a bit of a dodgy wicket, but he did bowl with a fair bit of pace.

Steve Garland: At school Nathan was a genuine all-rounder. He batted at four for us, and he usually opened the bowling. For his age he was reasonably sharp, and his accuracy, for which he became renowned, meant that he often got a good bunch of wickets.

Gary Stead was our captain as a fifth former, with Nathan in the side. We won third grade, division two, then third grade, division one, then made the second grade and won that. For about a decade we were probably the dominant team in Christchurch secondary school cricket.

I remember that in one Canterbury senior rep game we had seven former Shirley Boys' High School players in the team. I was very fortunate to have such quality guys coming through. It was a pleasure to be with them every Saturday. They understood the game, and they played such positive cricket.

Stephen Fleming: Shirley Boys' High School was regarded as a very strong school for producing cricketers. At Cashmere High we didn't have that tradition.

I had a lot of friends from Cashmere High in common with Nath, and we played an inter-school game where we cleaned up Shirley Boys' quite easily. They had the Steads and the Astles, a strong team, and we took great pleasure at that point in winning that game. A lot of my school friends who are overseas now often remind Nathan of that game.

But generally we were considered to be down the pecking order at Cashmere High, and I always felt that Shirley Boys' were very strong.

Steve Garland: Nathan was such a free-scoring batsman that he could win you games from nowhere. Of all the players we've had through here, I don't think there's been one other who had the natural hand-eye co-ordination Nathan had.

Some might say that he doesn't move his feet enough or that his technique wasn't quite fine enough. It never worried me, because his lack of technique in the old MCC way was never what got him out. Nathan would more often get himself out by being a bit too aggressive. A player like him is almost a freak, and you don't want to coach that natural flair out of him. Why would you want to hinder that type of ability?

If he'd been getting out regularly to one particular shot, I would have tried to change him. But that didn't happen. He was a super-positive batsman from the start. Most of his big innings were made up of singles, fours and sixes. Not a lot else. And it wasn't just big hitting — and he could belt it anywhere — it was such *clean* hitting. When you ask schoolboys to increase the tempo, quite often you find yourself three, four, five wickets down, and you've made no progress because they try to slog it. You didn't have to do that with Nathan. You just let him play his natural game.

He got criticised for being too free-scoring, and then there was a test match at Eden Park in 1997 where he batted all day for an unbeaten century, to save the game, and it was almost as if he was saying to his critics, 'You see, I can bat all day, bat defensively, if it's required'.

One of the lasting memories I have of him at school was

a game when we were into the top four of the competition, and we were playing Marist out at Ilam. He smashed them, and I mean smashed them, to all parts of the ground. He got 178, and Gary [Stead] was 93 not out. Gary did all he could to get Nathan on strike, and he'd be whacking them over mid-wicket from outside off; he was just amazing to watch. The fact that he could dominate a game like that to such a degree was sensational.

That was the sort of guy he was. In all of our inter-schools against Southland Boys' High and Kings' High from Dunedin, you could basically rely on him for a century. There were times, as in his international days, when he might get out early, but if he got in, you could guarantee he'd get a big score.

When he played cricket you felt that he was in an environment that he was completely at ease in, and later that was the same when he was playing in front of 30,000 or more people; it didn't phase him. On the other hand, a couple of years ago we asked him and Craig McMillan to speak at the school's sports awards dinner. They're similar in that they play in a quite aggressive way, but neither wanted to stand up and deliver a speech. Craig said, 'I don't mind playing in front of a sell-out crowd in Melbourne, that's okay, but put me in front of 130 school kids, and I'd just be a mess'. They were happy to do questions and answers, but the idea of a speech unsettled them.

It's a matter of comfort zones, isn't it? For Nathan and cricket, he was like a duck taking to water.

This Guy Can Play!

During the time I was at school Mum and Dad hammered me about doing my schoolwork, but they didn't try to push me into a profession or a trade. When I left school in the August holidays in my seventh-form year, I worked at Canterbury Sports Depot, run by Murray Smith, for about a year. It was a time when Murray was happy to let me have time off to play.

To be honest, I worked there largely because it was a shop involved with sport. At first I loved it, but then the novelty wore off, and although the people I worked with were great, I got bored with the job itself.

Other than sport, I had no idea what I wanted to do in my life and I guess that if the cricket hadn't taken off I might have ended up working there for who knows how long.

When I was 20, I had my first overseas trip with the Farsley club, near Leeds, in the Yorkshire league. I paid my own way there, and had to help look after the ground to earn my keep. There are a lot of people who are fascinated with turf care and preparing wickets, but I have to admit that I'm not one. For me, wickets are made to play on, not to organise the heavy roller for.

But it was very good for me to see just how much time and effort people put in to making a club run. It wasn't something that I'd thought much about as a young cricketer. Back then, it was a case of turning up, playing and then shooting off.

David Storr (Farsley Cricket Club chairman): I got to know about Nathan through Darren Gough, who would later play for England, when he visited me not long after he'd been playing club cricket in Christchurch.

He said, 'There's a guy in Christchurch called Nathan Astle, who is a really good striker of the cricket ball, and he's shown an interest in coming to play league cricket'.

I asked what he could do, and Darren said, 'Put it this way, he can bat a bit, he bowls medium pace, and he's a good athlete. He's worth getting in touch with.'

To cut a long story short, he came over, and he was a revelation. He stayed with me and my family for a couple of months until he found a flat. I remember him arriving on a Thursday evening; I picked him up, and we went for a drive up to the club. He wanted a knock there and then. I was still playing in the second XI, so I threw a few down, and he started smashing them here, there and everywhere. I think we might have even lost a couple of balls.

That Saturday, when he'd still really just got off the plane, he scored 120, maybe 130, in his first match, which was something of a sensation. He went on to score the most runs in the league that season.

We had him opening for us and with his great eye, he played the game the way it should be played. If the first ball he faced needed hitting for six, he hit it for six.

He didn't try to knock himself in, or play himself in, he was a very aggressive, very forthright batsman. Not like him as a person, he's actually a very introverted person. I found it hard to come to terms with the difference between this very quiet young man off the field and the man who was so sensational on it.

Our club president, who still is president, was the former England captain, Raymond Illingworth, who had begun his career with Farsley as a boy. We'd talk cricket with Nathan, and Nathan never used to say a great deal when Raymond was speaking, he was more of a listener, and seemed to prefer to do his talking with a bat when he was on the cricket pitch.

He was a very well-liked guy, and that doesn't seem to have changed. Four years ago I'd heard the New Zealanders were practising at Headingley on the Wednesday before a test. I helped raise funds for the club with an annual dinner where we auctioned cricket items. I took a bat with me to Headingley, hoping to get Nathan to sign it.

I was waiting when their coach arrived, and I wasn't sure if Nathan would recognise me. I was on crutches waiting for a hip replacement operation. He came straight up to me, asked how I was, and we had a really nice chat. I left the bat with him, and when we got it back he'd got it signed by both the New Zealand and the English team. I thought that was a really decent thing to do.

He's a nice guy. If you'll forgive me putting it in blunt Yorkshireman terms, he's not a guy that's up his own arse. I would have to say that there was only one really distressing thing about him then: he wouldn't have gravy on his Yorkshire pudding. How the hell do you have a man living in your house who doesn't have gravy on his meal? I ask you.

There's plenty of humour in league cricket, and one of the legendary tales you'll hear concerns a tubby Aussie called Cec Pepper, who they say went to live in England in the 1940s after abusing Don Bradman for not walking in a state game. In Lancashire, Pepper had been mercilessly chipping an umpire all day. He then started to get nervous about drawing an official complaint over his behaviour. Pepper went to the umpire, and said he hoped he hadn't taken what Pepper had been saying to heart.

'Not to worry,' said the ump. 'Up here we like a chap as speaks his mind.' Pepper was charmed. Next over he roared an appeal for a blatant lbw. The umpire smiled and said quietly, 'Not out, thee fat Australian bastard'. Later, I went to Accrington, north of Manchester, in the Lancashire league. I was there twice, once in 1998, when they let me cut the season short when I was asked to play for Nottinghamshire, and then for a full season in 2000.

Damien Clarke (Accrington team-mate): Nathan and Kelly came in 2000, and right from the start they fitted in very well. The difference Nathan made to the club was that people were keen to play in the team with him, and when they did play they didn't want to let him down. We had lads who wanted to impress in our second team, so they could get the chance to play alongside him. You could say it made people pull their socks up a bit more.

We got our money's worth from him. (Laughs.) There were some games where Nathan bowled 25 overs. We finished in the top half of the table that year, which was the best result we'd had for some time. To be honest, it's better than how we've done since.

League cricket has been around for nearly 120 years up north, and right from the start the clubs have had a professional on board.

All the clubs own their grounds, which are very picturesque — most of them having been well established for many years — and very well looked after. Most of the clubs seem to be run very, very well. They all have their own clubhouses, and after the game there's always a few beers, which makes it a lot of fun. They do drink beer very well in the north of England.

You don't have to travel far to play, never more than an hour's drive and the clubs are very family oriented. That means that if your dad played for a club, that's almost certainly going to be the one you'll play for. So it stays close-knit.

Because each club has its own ground, playing there is hugely different from, say, playing club cricket in Christchurch, where on a Saturday the ropes marking the boundaries overlap and you're standing next to a guy fielding at fine leg in his game while you're at mid-off in yours.

The 50-over games — all played on Sundays, starting at 1 p.m., when the non-professionals can get time off — are played seriously, but obviously not at the level of county cricket. Although it's the social highlight of the week for a lot of the local guys, they don't like losing, so they play to win.

Think of a senior club team in New Zealand, with one paid cricketer, often an international, involved. Over the years they've had Shane Warne, Clive Lloyd, Steve Waugh and Kapil Dev playing in the league. The rules are different for the professional. The pro is allowed to bowl 25 of the 50 overs, so the clubs get full value from their pros.

It's pretty homely, but that's not to say that the standard is mediocre. The people who only play league cricket are very competent, and it appeared to me that the young players who went into county cricket virtually all came from the leagues, so it was a good stepping stone for them. I remember in the Lancashire league in the Burnley club a young guy called Jimmy Anderson, a fast bowler, who we played against, who progressed very quickly into the England team.

And although a lot of the local players won't progress further up the ladder, that's not really the point. They're competitive, but the main reason they're playing cricket is for the fun. Just as a New Zealand club team does, they train twice a week, and then have the game on Sunday. The pro will usually take the practices.

At times, I wondered about teams relying so heavily on their professional player. With the professional being allowed to bowl 25 overs, it could get to a point where the game was largely pro versus pro, which can't have been great for the young guys trying to improve their game. I can certainly remember bowling my 25 overs a couple of times, and I usually bowled from 15 to 20 overs per game, so I guess you could say they got their fair share of bowling out of me. As well as bowling, the pro is also expected to pretty much win the game with his batting. I guess that that's the job the professional player is being asked to do; but I do think it'd be better for the local players if they limited the numbers of overs any player could bowl.

Apart from that, I found league cricket to be great, the sort of cricket you can't help but enjoy. The people up north are very hospitable, and they enjoy their time on the pitch and off it. They really love their cricket, and they don't just have one team, most of the clubs have five or six grades. Good-sized crowds turn out as well, and when someone gets a 50 or a hundred, or five wickets, someone else in the team goes round with a little wooden box, and they collect for the player who has done well on the day. Usually the money goes back on the bar.

There's a real family feel to it. From grandparents to kids, they turn up to watch, and as a player you even chuck in a couple of pounds for tea and sandwiches between innings. You all eat afternoon tea together. Then at the end of the day everyone goes back to the clubhouse to have a beer and a yarn. It's a bit like a trip back in time, with ladies in the kitchen getting the tea ready.

When I came back to Canterbury, I was lucky enough to get my old job back at the sports shop. My cricket was going well, but playing for New Zealand was something very much in the back of my mind. There was never a blinding flash of light, a voice in my head saying, 'You will play for New Zealand'. It's the dream we all have in sport, playing for your country, but for me it happened as a natural progression, not in a sudden, earth-shattering burst.

I was very fortunate in that I didn't have to sacrifice anything to get my chances in cricket. Before I was a professional player I was lucky enough to be able to play and keep my job. With the time I had off, I was getting picked in rep teams, first at age group, and then at senior level, and I just kept going.

My living came from the sports shop, where I was getting about $180 a week. Early on, for the first four or five months that I was working, Mum and Dad let me stay at home for free, and then they started charging me something like $20 a week. It wasn't a huge amount. Dad let me borrow his 'bogan' work van a few times, a white Escort with lights on top, and blue and green painted stripes. But then I moved up to a classy orange-coloured Datsun Sunny that cost me about $1200.

In those days, it was common to spend a lot of time in summer at your cricket club. We'd practise on a Tuesday or a Thursday night, but I wasn't one who did extra things on my own, the club nights were basically it for me. In the weekend you'd play your game, then stay there, at the club, for a while. I think that's largely gone now, but then, in the late 1980s, it was mainly the guys at the East Shirley cricket team that I'd stay and have a drink with, and, of course, if you were playing away, you'd stay at the club you'd played. So my social life revolved around my sport and it was a big part of my life.

When I left school, I kept in touch with a couple of guys, but

I wouldn't say they were my best friends. As time went by, the closest friendships were with my mates from cricket.

In the week leading up to being selected for the Canterbury side, in 1991, the Canterbury coach, David Trist, had been to see our games over a couple of weekends. We were all aware that he was there, although none of us knew who exactly he was interested in watching. Then Tristy told me he wanted me to play one-day cricket for Canterbury.

Tristy is a Christchurch born and raised man, although with the moustache, his snappy dressing, love of wine and conversation, and the amount of time he's spent coaching in South Africa, Holland, and Hong Kong, it'd be easy to believe he grew up in a European city. He had a brief, but lively, career as a fast bowler for Canterbury and New Zealand in the late 1960s and '70s, touring to India with a New Zealand side before he'd played for Canterbury. But coaching was where he really made his mark. I didn't know Tristy before getting into the Canterbury team. Some people say he's eccentric, but I'd be more inclined to simply say that he's different, more openly enthusiastic than a lot of coaches.

David Trist: I'd not long come back from South Africa, where I'd coached Eastern Province. It was quite a tumultuous time, with apartheid nearing an end, and rebel tours. I'd coached Kepler Wessells, and got him to come over, and then, after one rebel tour he played for Australia, which was even more challenging to a lot of the South African players. (Laughs.) Mostly to those who couldn't get his money.

Then I came back to Canterbury, so I didn't have great background knowledge of the young stars coming through. Stephen Fleming stuck out, and he went almost immediately into the team after I returned. I felt I was extraordinarily lucky, I fell onto this young group of guys who were having fun on and off the field. To me it looked like I couldn't miss. People were saying, 'Aw, Canterbury are crap. They haven't won a title for 20 years.' And I was thinking, 'Well, if we can't win games with this mob, I'm bloody useless, and they aren't what I think they are'.

Nathan had been quite a star at Shirley Boys' High, and although he wasn't in that initial first year, one or two players who I respected said he was worth looking at. I always listened to what players said, because, after all, they bowl to him or bat to him.

Nathan came in on the recommendation of Stephen Fleming, and, I think, Chris Cairns, who kept urging me to go and have a look myself. I went and I remember thinking, 'Yeah, he's good, but how do I fit him into the side?'. At that stage we had Chris Harris batting at No. 7, Mark Priest at No. 8, getting runs, Richard Petrie, holding a bat, trying to claim he was a batsman, and so Nathan played more or less as a bowler who batted.

He batted at nine, which startled him, I'm sure, but he never said anything. I didn't know enough about him, so although I knew he was a batsman, I really liked his bowling. In the conditions you get in New Zealand around Christmas time, where it swings and seams a little bit, I thought, 'He'll do a good job for us'.

Gary Stead: That was an interesting thing with Nathan then, coming into that side as a bowler, batting at No. 9. In those days they often played at Hagley Park, with really low, slow wickets, and Nathan would bowl his 10 overs for 20. Almost the Gavin Larsen type of bowler. But I used to look at it when it came time to bat, and think, 'Gee, I hope he gets a chance a bit higher up soon'.

Stephen Fleming: For me it was his batting that stuck in my mind early on, at school and in club cricket, but he bowled a bit, and they were probably pretty equal in the early days. Then, almost by accident, he got his chance to get into the Canterbury side as a bowler. But to me, batting and bowling were always in parallel.

I know that when he first got into the Canterbury team it was for his bowling, and his batting was seen as a bonus, which I'm not sure was reading it the right way. It just panned out that way. He just had to get the chance to show how well he could bat. When he was playing for Canterbury B he would bowl a little bit, and his statistics were so good he'd be asked to bowl a bit more, and he then put such good numbers up for his bowling that he was seen as an option for the one-day team especially.

Geoff Allott: A point I'd really like to stress is that the one aspect people haven't respected enough about Nathan is his bowling. As a fellow bowler there was nothing better than coming on and bowling with Nath at the other end. It's a part of his game that I don't think has been exploited enough and hasn't had the recognition it deserves.

Probably because in the later stages of his career he had a back injury that limited how much he bowled, it gets, to a degree, forgotten. But he had a tremendous record as a bowler. His runs per over rate was phenomenal.

His accuracy was a result of his physical gifts and his discipline. His accuracy was amazing, and he developed a tremendous use of the slower ball. He had an ability to reverse swing the ball, which wasn't commonly seen in New Zealand, and was something I think could have been exploited more.

If you go back and look at slow-motion shots, his presentation of the seam was outstanding, and that was why he'd get a little bit of nip when others might not.

Gary Stead (Canterbury and Black Caps team-mate): One of the reasons I think Nathan was so successful was that he kept it very, very simple. He'd never complicate it too much. I think he would listen to other people, but he had his own way of developing himself.

He's had a lot of coaches, but I think he's the kind of guy who thinks, 'No, this is the way I'm going to bat, and I'll stick to it'. And he's a forthright, stubborn person in that area. For a pleasant, quiet sort of guy he can be extremely stubborn. Nathan's not a loner at all, but if you see him in a group, he's never the loud one. He sits back, and he listens, and I think he takes in a lot more than some people give him credit for at times.

In the end he makes up his own mind. He either picks up what someone is saying, or, if he doesn't agree, basically goes, 'Thanks for talking, but I think you're talking bullshit'. He makes that sort of decision fairly quickly.

David Trist: I'd gone from the Canterbury scene in 1993, and it was quite clear that, along with several others, Nathan was going to make it through to the New Zealand side.

He was never one who stood out to me in the nets, or one who pushed his own case. When he began, his support came from players, who would tell me, 'This guy can play'. It made you keep looking at him, wondering if you should move him up the order. Later on when he became an opener, and I had a bit of a Glenn Turner approach to one-day cricket — which was that it was better to be bowled out by the last ball, having

The Kid: Nathan the new baby and boxing champion, who also happily shared a rug with his brother, and a swing (as he later would his cricket), with sister Lisa.

Chris Cairns, 3½ years old.

Stephen Fleming, 10 years old.

Craig Spearman, 12 years old.

Nathan Astle, 4 years old.

Who brings out the best in our young cricketers?

At Shell we're proud to support the future of New Zealand cricket.

You can be sure of Shell

This promotional poster from the 1990s includes a family shot of Nathan, at four years old, about to face a delivery from his dad.

Soccer was an early love. In this St Albans/Shirley team, Nathan is the 10-year-old sitting on the far right of the front row.

John and Lee Astle, parents who provided the perfect environment for sports-mad kids.

By his early teens Nathan was a Canterbury age group rep, adept with either the boot or his head.

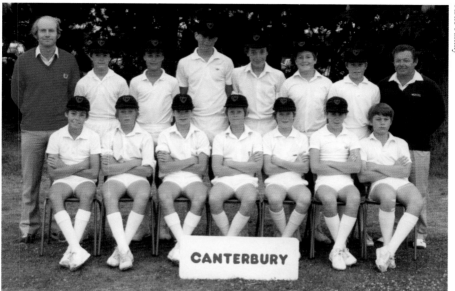

In the summer of 1984–85, the Canterbury Under 15 side had some big names of the future. That's Nathan next to the Chris Harris lookalike at the far left of the back row. Seated: far left is Stephen Fleming, second from right is Gary Stead, with Llorne Howell far right.

The teenaged Astles were all Canterbury age group representatives. Nathan in soccer and cricket, Lisa in cricket, and Daniel in table tennis.

A different taste of international cricket: playing for New Zealand in the Hong Kong Sixes in the early 1990s.

Astle Family

One of the most characteristic Nathan Astle shots, the square cut, was already firmly in place by the time he made the Canterbury one-day team.

The first black cap, awarded in 1996.

given it a real go, rather than be seven down, but miss the run-chase — Nathan was just allowed to play the way he wanted to play, and he was pretty much able to do it.

I was lucky, in a way, that there were a lot of bigger names than me in the Canterbury side, so I didn't have to try to develop under the spotlight. Because I was bowling a few overs, and batting at the tail, my introduction to the first-class scene was pretty low key. Playing for Canterbury didn't feel like a dramatic change to me, but I guess the fact that I wasn't under great pressure was an element in that.

Gary Stead: The Canterbury team of the 1990s was very much a home-grown side. There were a lot of people who came through together in the province. It was a special team in that one of the big goals was to get our people playing for New Zealand. To get that was almost as satisfying, certainly in my mind, as the success the team had in competition.

And I guess it was a special team because although no one had made it for New Zealand at that early stage, soon after you had a string of guys, Fleming, Germon, Harris, Astle, all these guys pushing through. It was something to do with the group of players we had, but also the coaching structures had to have played a part. We weren't all close friends in the side; I think some possibly didn't even especially like some of the others, but I do think everyone respected each other. Obviously with any team, not everybody's going to be the best of mates, but you had a whole group of people coming through of a similar age, so you had a lot of people with similar interests and aims.

You had some older players, like Mark Priest, who in a lot of ways reminded me of Nathan. Do your own job well and the team will look after itself. So while I don't think it was all exactly 'brothers in arms', what was important was that we respected each other, and we enjoyed each other's success.

Geoff Allott: To me, that time in the Canterbury team was some of the most enjoyable cricket I ever got to play. We all knew that everyone else in the team was going to perform. There was no negativity whatsoever. We all knew we had ability, almost in an arrogant way; but being Canterbury, it was controlled confidence. We didn't shout it out.

At the same time, inside the group, we just knew we were going to turn up and win games, and to have that sense in a side meant that everything we did was enjoyable. That included practice, fitness training, to turning up at the match and seeing the successes of individuals. If Nath and Flem didn't score hundreds, then Cairnsy did. If Cairnsy wasn't scoring well, then Darrin Murray or Lee Germon would.

Amongst ourselves, and only amongst ourselves, we used to refer to an annual game we had with Otago as the 'Boxing Day Massacre'. It didn't matter, we were going to turn up and annihilate them, and that was the confidence the side had.

We were all individuals, all with our own skill sets, all with our own roles to play inside the team. I'd give a lot of credit to David [Trist] and Denis [Aberhart] for that, because they identified it, and didn't try to change it. As a result of the success everyone was happy, and it was a terrific decade in Canterbury cricket.

The fact that most of us had played together at an early age meant we knew each other; a lot of us were mates, we knew what made people click, we knew what was happening in people's personal lives. To me, the foundation was laid through the experience of playing through the grades, and respecting the people who had already won higher honours, like Rod Latham. So then, when you have players who you aspire to be like, and you find yourself playing with them, and if your performance was as good, then you started to believe that you could make it to a higher level too.

So that wheel of success starts to roll, and players started being better than anyone else in the country. It was a great reward, but we also wanted other younger people coming in to see the success and emulate it themselves.

It's a long process that does start getting built at an early age. We've been very fortunate in Canterbury that we've had a stable group of players, who have encouraged younger players coming through. When you made the Canterbury team all you had to concentrate on was your cricket, you didn't have to worry about what a person was like in their private life; that was a given.

People, especially those outside Canterbury, often believe that there's some sort of instant bond in any sporting side from the province, that as soon as the red and black colours are put on you're blood brothers.

But, in those days, I actually found it quite daunting to be a young guy in the team. To a degree, there was certainly a system of seniority operating and as a new player you sat in the corner. The senior players had their spots in the shed, and you didn't go near them: they spoke to you, you didn't speak to them. For a young kid, it could be quite nerve-wracking.

What helped the nerves was that in the early 1990s the experienced players, the New Zealand players, still played club cricket, and because you'd played against them several times in club cricket, you felt as if you knew them. Of course, at times you'd have done well against them and that helps you feel at ease when you come into a team as a younger player. There was also the fact that some of the players were people like Flem, and Llorne Howell, who I knew, so I wasn't there by myself.

But I should also make it clear, that while the players who had been in the team for a while were old school, they were also very helpful. While I was learning the ropes, it wasn't an initiation that was unpleasant or mean-spirited. There were formalities, but there wasn't mental cruelty. They just had a line that, at the age you were, you didn't cross. You respected that. Personally, I don't think it's a bad thing. As long as the more experienced players treat younger guys with some sort of respect, then I believe it's like any sport, or any job for that matter, you have to do your time to get to the top.

Tristy had a good handle on the older-younger mix, and he was able to manage that very well, getting us all working for the same thing. Another thing that helped me relax in those early days were guys like Stu Roberts, Chris Flanagan and Peter Kennedy, who were always a lot of fun.

They were always doing silly things in the changing shed like hiding guys' cricket coffins, hiding gloves, or wrecking someone's coffins. They came across as regular guys, which helps a 20-year-old playing at provincial level for the first time. They gave it something of the feel of a club team.

We'd play silly games, like one we called cricket-tennis, where you'd have a couple of coffins in the middle of the changing room, a player at each end with a cricket bat, and you'd smash hell out of the cricket ball, hitting it over the coffins. Guys like Stuey Roberts and Peter Kennedy wouldn't back away from trying to hurt people.

By the time I got into the Canterbury team I'd reached a stage where I basically knew what my game was. Tristy would help if it was needed, and guys like Rod Latham and Blair Hartland would chip in and help out if I wanted something.

David Trist: He never came to me in a nasty or aggressive way to say, 'What the hell is going on here?'. It was obvious that several other players thought he should be batting higher, and I guess I was quite old in relation to this very young, but supercharged, group of guys, so they didn't want to challenge me directly.

But in subtle ways they encouraged me to change my view. In the very early stages of his career we played Auckland at Eden Park in 1992, and they then had virtually the New Zealand line-up of fast bowlers. They knocked us over, and Nathan top scored with 37 in the first innings, playing his natural way, quite boldly, and he got some runs in the second innings as well.

It became obvious that he would have to bat further up the order. So it was by making use of the opportunities he did have, that he was able to push his way forward. I was guilty of initially not recognising his batting qualities. But I hope that Nathan might say, 'Well, at least I got to play'.

It was a wonderful time to be with Canterbury. When we had that final against Wellington in 1992 at Jade Stadium there were 25,000 people there. When we had a testimonial match for Rod Latham, over 20,000 people turned up. You wouldn't get that for a one-day international now. It was a very exciting time, and Nathan became part of that, and not long after he started playing for New Zealand.

In general, there was a good team feel. In any team there'll always be the guys you're comfortable with, that you'll spend free time with, and for me that was Flem, Llorne Howell and Michael Owens, who I'd been with in youth teams.

It was an exciting time. As a young guy, travelling with people your own age, playing your cricket, but also going out at night, it was a lot of fun. You realise that you're a lucky person to be able to have a job that's so different from a nine-to-five job; you're doing something you love and making a living from it. What could be better? Looking back, it's that situation where you're a bit like a kid in a candy store; whether it's the travel, or getting new gear, it's all stuff you enjoy.

It was an odd feeling too, getting attention from the media. To pick up the paper and find a story about yourself, even the occasional interview, was definitely a novelty for a while. You'd be lying to say that it didn't feel pretty cool to look in the paper and see your name with a score beside it. You remembered the days when you'd always look for the New Zealand scores, or the Canterbury scores, to see who got runs, and now, finally, it's your name that's there.

I was treated pretty fairly by the media when I started out. I was lucky enough to be in a side that was winning a lot, and that doesn't carry a lot of bad press with it. There were personalities in the team a lot bigger than I was, so I think I had two or maybe three years where most of the attention was on the other guys. Someone like Cairnsy, who was always tagged because he was Lance Cairns's son, was under the microscope all the time. I was fortunate enough to be in the background, and do my thing, which made it a nice slow progression into my career.

On the pitch there were times when I found myself bowling to Martin Crowe, probably the best batsman ever for New Zealand, or found myself facing guys like Gavin Larsen, who I used to go and watch playing for New Zealand. I'd get a bit nervous, but balancing that was a feeling of excitement that goes with playing against, or with, guys who are world-class players.

As a kid, I idolised Ian Botham and Vivian Richards, so I was hoping to play the game as they did, but there was no New Zealander who I was obsessed with. When I was very small, just six years old, Mum and Dad took me to a sports store in Christchurch, and now we have a photo of me sitting on Botham's knee. In the years since, I've had the opportunity to have a couple of meals and a few wines with him, so I've had the chance to get to know him a bit. I've even had a game of golf with him, and he's a very accommodating guy, who is full of exuberance and good fun.

I've met Vivian Richards in the West Indies a couple of times, but I've never had a yarn with him. But as time progressed, the player who stuck out a mile for me was Martin Crowe. He was one of those guys who, at his peak, was one of the best in the world. The older I got, the more I looked up to him, as did a lot of young cricketers in New Zealand. He was the benchmark.

Up with the Best

You could say that my mate Stephen Fleming helped get me my first taste of international cricket. When I got the call, in January 1995, to say I was in the one-day squad to play a three-game series with the West Indies, Flem was one of the first people I rang. The conversation took a funny turn almost straight away. I called him and said, 'Yay, we'll be playing together'. And he said, 'Yay, no we won't be'. I initially had no idea what he was talking about.

Stephen Fleming: When Nathan was first picked for the New Zealand side he rang up and said, 'I've just found out I've been picked, and we'll be playing together in the New Zealand side'.

At that point, I knew I was going to be suspended, along with Dion Nash and Matthew Hart, for smoking marijuana at a team barbecue in South Africa, but it hadn't been announced. I had been hoping that I might get away with a fine, and we could play together. It was a massive disappointment to me that we couldn't play his first game together.

We made up for it, playing for New Zealand together later, but although he doesn't talk about the history of the game much, he does bring that up from time to time..

With hindsight, I suppose I really did get the chance because the three guys had been suspended. The call to play for New Zealand had come as something of a surprise. At that time they had a reasonably solid middle, with Chris Cairns, Shane Thomson, and, of course, Flem. When you look at it, guys like Dion Nash and Matthew Hart, pretty much did what I did, bowled and batted, so the suspension logically had to have something to do with it.

Moving from club cricket to Canterbury hadn't felt like such a big step, but going from Canterbury to New Zealand certainly was. Instead of being alongside guys I'd played club cricket with in Canterbury — and had a few drinks with after a club game — I was in a changing room with the likes of Martin Crowe, Gavin Larsen, Dipak Patel and Danny Morrison, players who had been around for a while. Some of them, I'd watched as a kid, and now I was sitting next to them in the shed.

At that time there was definitely a pecking order. It was a kind of unwritten rule that you knew your place, and it was almost a case of only speaking to them if they spoke to you. I say almost the case, and I'm not saying they were awful guys at all, but when you're a young kid, going in there new, you take your time, and tread pretty carefully. In a new environment, I'm a reasonably shy sort of person anyway. I won't make a lot of racket or chew someone's ear off. I'll be more inclined to go about my business quietly.

At that time, Glenn Turner was the coach, and as far as his coaching nous and his knowledge of the game, I'd put him second to none. I thought he was brilliant as far as reading a game goes, and he also understood players very well from a technical perspective. He could analyse what a player was doing very quickly, but he didn't try to change your basic game. He adapted things to the technique of the men he had.

He wasn't a pushy coach, hammering you with his opinion, he was very much a guy who if you wanted answers you went to him, and he'd tell you what you wanted. He promoted self-reliance, getting to know your own game better, rather than being in your ear the whole time, telling you what you should be doing.

His view was that you should learn to sort out your own game. Then, if there was something you were struggling with, you could see him, have a yarn, and he would usually come up with a pretty good answer. I was new to the team, a young guy trying to do my best, but I found that, despite his reputation for being quite severe, Glenn was actually a man with a very dry sense of humour, and once you got to know him, he's a funny guy, a good person to sit down and have a talk with.

There was criticism of him when he was a captain, and later as a coach, for not being encouraging enough, and never showering players with praise. But what that meant to me, was that if he did come to you and say, 'Well done', then you knew without doubt that you'd done very well. He took the view that it was our job — and it is, it's what we're paid for — to get runs and take wickets.

I'm a bit the same. It's always nice if someone comes up and says congratulations or well done: it does make you feel good. But when it comes down to it, it is our job, and that's what's expected of us. That was pretty much the way he coached.

Glenn Turner (New Zealand coach 1995–1996): We saw Nathan as an underestimated all-rounder, really. He could certainly bat, but his bowling in limited overs was not to be underestimated either. He did a damn good job throughout his career as a useful one-day bowler, and he did come into the all-round category very much.

Particularly if you played on pitches that were a bit low and slow, his type of bowling was more than useful. I felt that in the middle to late 1990s, especially, he was our best all-rounder in limited overs, and he wasn't given credit for that. Generally, in the 1990s, Nathan got 100 off 120 deliveries, which was certainly good enough to win those games. And most all-rounders don't do enough with either the bat or the ball individually to win the game.

They can certainly make a major contribution towards a win when you combine the two efforts, but so many all-rounders can't get a hundred, or not quickly enough, or they can't take five wickets, or they can't bowl their 10 overs for less than 4.5 runs an over. Whereas, someone who specialises a bit more in one area than the other, can be a matchwinner in one area, and still be very useful with the other skill. That was where I saw him.

He was a batsman who didn't show the full face of the bat for a long period of time through the shot. So his timing needed to be critical. When he was slightly out of nick, he killed a lot of shots by closing the blade too early, and so the mistiming would come about.

But when his timing was on, he could hit the ball from closer to the off stump, further behind point than most, because of that point of impact being much later. That was a skill he had. I know opposing teams started to cut it off a little bit, by putting a couple of fielders, or even more, behind point.

He's right in saying that he wasn't totally orthodox. He had his own way of playing. But a lot of people do, and you never want to coach someone out of that. It's crazy to try. I try to encourage everyone to, not so much take a lot of risks at the crease, but more to make sure that they keep busy. It's to be more active, to look to attack first, and defend second. It's a basic mind-set that is always aware that you can't afford to abuse time. It doesn't mean that you can't give yourself time to start judging the pace and the bounce and playing yourself in, but whilst you're doing that you need to be scoring.

There's nothing worse than batsmen going to the crease, even if you're opening, let alone in the middle of the innings, and batting for 20 balls for two runs, and then getting out. You've still got a chance of getting out at that point, after 20 or so balls, and if you get three or four batsmen in your side who do that, you just can't get the sort of total you need.

So what I'm saying is, when you first go in, look to get bat on ball, look to manoeuvre it somewhere while you're getting yourself established. If you get a gimme, obviously you can still put it away, whether it's first or second ball.

The important thing is not being totally scoreless during those early stages of an innings. With Nathan, because he played the ball so late, and the way that his hands worked, with the field up, and hitting the ball quite square, especially on the off side, you don't have to be that wide of the fielder to actually beat them.

Because they don't have sweepers in during those early overs, it meant he was more likely to get full benefit from his bigger shots. So the boundaries tended to come quite early for him.

My first trip overseas with the Black Caps was to India, late in 1995. I was in the one-day squad to play a six-game series. As it happened, one game was eventually abandoned because it was washed out, but India won the series 3–2.

It was the last time Martin Crowe would play for New Zealand. Comparing him to other batters around the world, he was definitely one of the best, and I don't think we saw as much of Martin on the international stage as we all would have liked.

Having played with him, as well as having watched him on television, it seems to me that if his knee hadn't packed up on him, his stats would have been even better than they were, and they were already outstanding.

I would have loved the chance to have played with him more. A great player like Martin is someone you can learn a lot from just by watching how he approaches things, how he goes about his batting; time playing with him could mean so much to a young player starting out.

Martin is a highly strung sort of guy, which was reflected in the perfection that he was always seeking in his cricket. His intensity was so great that it may almost have been a downfall at times. He must have found it very hard to deal with players who weren't as intense as he was. But once you got to know him, he's a very genuine, hell of a nice guy, an interesting character and a very independent thinker, who could be considered temperamental because of that.

Over the years, I've given him a few phone calls, just to talk over batting techniques. He had said to me, and to a couple of other guys, including Flem, that if we ever wanted to call him to talk over anything, or wanted to get his ideas, not to be afraid to give him a ring. Looking back, I think I may have underutilised his offer of help.

On very rare occasions he would come in for a session with the Black Caps, but I can't understand why a man of his stature in the game wasn't used a lot more. At the moment I think he's a wonderful resource that doesn't get used by cricket in New Zealand, which, to me, is a shame for a man of such huge talent.

Martin Crowe: In what I knew to be my last innings, at Nagpur, in a one-day game against India, Nathan and I put on a few runs (128 for the second wicket). He got his first one-day hundred (114).

In a sense, it was a bit of a handing over, in that it was my last game and he kicked off what would be a flurry of hundreds for New Zealand in one-day matches. We didn't really get to know each other then, but out in the middle I did see at first hand the natural talent he had.

When I finished as a player, I came back into the fray when Steve Rixon used me as batting consultant a year or so later. At that stage I had a chance to talk with Nathan about things like being more defensively solid at the crease, especially in test cricket, opening up the on side a little bit more, especially driving and the pull shot, so that he wasn't a one-dimensional off side player, when he had a natural bent for the off side.

He had a pretty good technical basis from the start. His stance was a little closed off in that it tended to line up the off side, extra cover, more than it did down the ground.

But it wasn't hard to get him to understand that if he opened his hips a little bit, and got his head pointing more at the bowler, he could hit down the ground, and through the on side, and therefore defend straighter.

It wasn't hard to get Nathan to see that if he did those things, he could be a more complete player. If you wanted to quantify it in tests, he probably went from a 30 average player, to the average he actually achieved [37.02 in tests]. In summary, he was an easy student, actually a lot easier to work with than Flem, who complicated it a lot more.

When I retired my knee was gone, and the body was starting to follow. (Laughs.) The only scenario that could have kept me going was to keep captaining the test team for a couple of years, and give up one-day cricket. That would have been less taxing on the body.

But Glenn Turner at the time decided that wasn't the right way forward. It had never been attempted before, so I just basically retired on the spot.

I tried to keep in touch with Nathan and Flem through the net sessions, which was not the best way, because I think the best way to coach is at the other end in a game. But that was the next best thing. He embraced that opportunity, although in the last few years I would have liked to have had more calls from him, because there were elements I could see from the commentary box that could have been easily corrected.

When he retired, I said publicly that I'll miss the fearlessness he brought to the game, and I will.

My first full tour with the Black Caps was to the West Indies in 1996. It began in March and ended, two months later, in controversy, when Adam Parore and Chris Cairns left before the tour was over. I was very disappointed with the way they left the tour. Whether Cairnsy was seriously injured or not, I can't say. I wasn't behind the scenes and wasn't privy to the reasons as to why he went and exactly what happened. I was pretty disappointed though.

Adam Parore's actions speak for themselves, I think. He was a talented cricketer, but as far as a person goes, some of the stuff he did, leaving when he did, summed him up. He was a very self-centred sort of guy. Having said that, I was probably more disappointed with Cairnsy. As far as Adam going, I could live with that pretty easily, but it seemed funny to me for Cairnsy to just get up in the middle of a tour like that and leave.

I then heard stories of him going back to play for Notts, so it was a tough one. He was on the way so quickly after he injured his side. A lot of the guys will hang round if they get injured and try to get the injury corrected. All I can remember is that I was batting in the nets in Barbados with Flem, and we were facing Cairnsy. It was some of the quickest bowling I have ever faced. I guess he was letting off some steam. That was when he pulled the muscles in his side. I remember talking to Flem in the nets and we were more or less effing and blinding, saying, 'Bloody hell, this is pretty quick'.

The tour was run along very authoritarian lines. As a newcomer, the biggest problem I could see was that you had Glenn as the coach, Gren Alabaster as manager, and Lee Germon as captain, and my take was that they were all exactly the same as personalities. Where Glenn let himself down a little was in his people management skills. They weren't that great. Gren Alabaster was of pretty much the same makeup, and so was Lee.

To me a good coaching mix was when we had Steve Rixon and John Graham. You had Steve who was a tough coach — you went out and you did the business, that was that. But then you had John Graham, who was tough, but very fair, and had a great way with people. That's where things fell down in the West Indies. There was a lot of, 'This is the way we're going to do it. If you don't agree with it, that's just tough luck.'

Looking back I think that if Glenn's manager had been DJ Graham, or Jeff Crowe, then a lot of the difficulties would have been avoided. If Glenn had had someone at his side who could have managed people better, I think he would have been an outstanding coach.

For me, the tour of the West Indies was certainly an interesting one. I can remember all of us sitting in a room round a big table shaped like a horseshoe with Glenn, Lee and Gren at the top of the table and the rest of the team facing them. It was then pretty much a big slanging match. You had guys, senior players, who wanted to do things the way they wanted. I don't mean run off and go their own way, stay out all night or that sort of thing, but how they went about training and so on.

Late the previous year I'd had a taste of how the Turner regime could be. We were touring India, and I'd joined for the one-day games at the end of tour. We had a barbecue with the New Zealand television crew. There was a swimming pool at the hotel, and we were all having a few beers as no games were scheduled for three or four days. A few people got thrown into the swimming pool, and later a few of us, including me, headed out. I remember that we tried to get into a nightclub, but they wouldn't let us in, so we ended up back at the hotel.

The next day at training, we were all sitting down, and Glenn came up and said, 'If I read your name out, go to the left, the rest stay where you are'. He went through and read out six or seven names, mine being one, and we went to the left. He said, 'Right, you guys I've just called out, you'll stay here and do a fitness session for an hour and a half, the rest may leave and go back to the hotel'.

Then he explained that he thought out of the whole team we were the ones who had had too much to drink, and we were getting punished for it. So we did about 90 minutes of fitness training, then went back in the afternoon to do our nets.

The funny thing was that there were a couple of guys in the group that went back to the hotel who had been out drinking just as much as we were, and one of them had been rooming with Lee Germon, but he got away with it.

Personally, I always got on reasonably well with Lee. He did suffer sometimes from having a cutting, sarcastic edge to him on the cricket field, and the issue for some guys, I'm sure, is that he didn't have any apprenticeship in the New Zealand side before he became captain. From his first game for New Zealand, he was the captain.

Some of the experienced guys may have looked at him and thought that Lee wasn't the outstanding player in his position, given that Adam Parore was so well rated internationally. They then may have found it hard to take orders from someone they didn't rate as much as themselves. I think there would have been a lot more support if Lee had made it clear that he would do his own thinking and, if need be, take a stand if he felt it was necessary. But there wasn't any sign of that, that I can remember, so he was seen largely as a Glenn Turner puppet.

I'd played under Lee for Canterbury for a couple of years before he captained New Zealand, and I was a little disappointed when he was leading New Zealand that he didn't stamp his own mark on the team. My feeling is that if you're asked to be captain, then you say, 'Well, I may not be here for very long, but I'll have a fair crack at it, do things my way, and leave something that I'm happy with'.

The impression I got was that he was pretty much doing what he was told by Glenn, and knowing from the Canterbury days what a strong character Lee could be, I was a little bit surprised that he couldn't say, 'No, I'll rely on my opinion a bit more'.

Whether he would have been allowed to, I suppose, is another story. I felt that both Lee and Gren Alabaster were having their strings pulled by Glenn; that it was his way or the highway. I very much felt that the whole management team was being directed by Glenn, who's a strong character with strong opinions.

So for me the West Indies trip wasn't so great a tour from the team side of it, and behind the scenes it was a real eye-opener. But it was my first big tour, we got through it, and had a bit of fun ourselves.

Glenn Turner: The people who seemed to have difficulties with me never came to my door, they never asked questions, never challenged anything. They went behind the scenes, they found the weakness there.

Nathan was as easy as hell — he didn't have the same ego some of the others did, he wasn't a bully, and he didn't want to take over things. He was ideal. He got on with his job. The problem that tends to arise is that you'll always get two or three in every side who want to coach, and manage, and select the side, and that's their personalities.

Nathan was ideal in that he was there to bat and bowl, and get on with his cricket, and he got on with it. If anything, I'd have sooner that he'd knocked on my door or challenged things more, but at least he wasn't going behind your back, trying to undermine you. There were no issues there at all.

I guess what tends to happen in a team situation is that the stronger personalities can lead a group, and if he went with the flow, I wouldn't blame him for that.

There was a big change at the top of New Zealand cricket after the West Indies tour. Christopher Doig took over as chief executive from Graham Dowling, Steve Rixon was appointed coach of the Black Caps, John Graham became the manager, and Flem replaced Lee Germon as captain.

Personally, I think it was a change that was needed, and from that point on things changed completely, for the better, and I think you've got to give a lot of credit to Christopher Doig. I know there were a few eyebrows raised at the time, people wondering what an opera singer was doing running New Zealand cricket, but I have a lot of admiration for what he did for the game in New Zealand. His enthusiasm was tremendous, and with marketing man Neil Maxwell he also brought a lot more money into the game. In a way, Chris made cricket attractive again to the public.

After what had happened in the West Indies he knew that he

needed two pretty strong characters to run the team, and the appointment of Steve Rixon and John Graham was outstanding. They complemented each other brilliantly. John was a former All Black captain, and head of Auckland Grammar School, who came with a reputation as a strict disciplinarian. We found that he was firm when he needed to be firm. You knew not to cross the line with DJ when he was getting his point across. He'd let you know in no uncertain terms if you weren't doing the right thing.

But he's also a man with a big heart, who would do anything for you, if you were struggling. I got on very, very well with him, and in fact, after he was out of the management role, he was toastmaster at my wedding.

I've kept in touch with him, and have a huge amount of respect for him, for what he did with the team. He brought in some pretty strict rules. We had to shave every day, we had a dress code we had to stick to. For a while it actually was like going back to school. We argued until we were blue in the face with him initially, but he didn't budge one bit, and in the years that he was manager, it did a lot of good for the team.

I can't speak highly enough of him. Even if you'd had a pretty fierce argument with him, when it finished, that was it. He never held a grudge. You could then have a beer with him, and carry on. He always respected your point of view. He would listen, but in the end the final decision rested with him, and he was never worried about making that decision. It would always be what he felt was best for the team, never just to score a cheap point — he was too big a man to ever do that. With DJ everything was straight up, he'd just say it as it was.

Steve Rixon was a coach I enjoyed immensely. He had a very basic philosophy: work hard, play hard, and enjoy yourself. He was a pretty tough coach. When he came on board our fielding improved out of sight. Some days he'd run us into the ground

— and it could possibly be argued that occasionally he ran us too hard too close to a game. But he was a perfectionist with the fielding. We'd stay out there until we got 10 out of 10. If we didn't get that, we'd go back to nought and start again. He brought a competitive edge into our training. But it was a fun competitive edge, which, unfortunately, was lost in the last few years, when fielding training became a little bit mundane and boring.

Every day with 'Stumper' he'd have a new game or drill. It'd take us five or ten minutes sometimes to grasp it, because Stumper would be there, his moustache quivering, firing out instructions. 'You-go-there, you-go-there, you-go-there, now, do-this, do-this, do-this.' If you didn't get it right he'd be standing there, yelling at the top of his lungs until you got it right. He'd come up with some quirky little games, always with two teams opposing each other, which really sharpened our competitive edge. I certainly enjoyed that. We were all competitive guys, which meant we liked challenging each other.

Stumper loved the game of cricket and he was endlessly enthusiastic. He was full of energy, which made him an awful cricket watcher; he could never just sit down and watch quietly. He'd sit down, get up, stomp around, and you could always tell when he wasn't happy with what was going on. He'd go bright red in the face, and everyone would be waiting for him to let rip. And he did let rip a few times, but once he had done that, it was over. Like DJ, he didn't carry grudges.

The time when DJ and Stumper were there, with guys like Dion Nash as well, was when a lot of us learnt to take things on the chin. We learned that if there was criticism, it wasn't because they were trying to put you down, nor were they trying to belittle you, they were trying to help you to get better. In general, I think New Zealanders are inclined to take things too personally, instead of sitting down, thrashing it out, and moving on.

Stumper was very much a man's man. He was always happy to sit down and have a yarn, have a drink, go out and have a little flutter on the horses. He was happy for you to enjoy yourself as well. As long as you turned up the next day and gave it 100 per cent he had no problem with how you relaxed.

He was big on enjoying each other's company at the end of the day, getting together in the bar, and getting to know each other better. There's not a real drinking culture in the team now anyway, but under John Bracewell I always had the impression that going out for a few drinks was basically frowned upon. Stumper had no problem with your social life, as long as it was under control to the point where you could always turn up the next day and do your job.

He was the man who started the era of the Black Caps being known as one of the best fielding teams in the world. You can definitely put that down to him. At training he had a cut–down bat, cut pretty much straight down the middle, and his skill with that, being able to put a cricket ball where he wanted to, was remarkable. For someone like myself, who often fielded in the slips, it was the perfect training for practising taking nicks.

Steve Rixon (New Zealand coach 1996–1999): Just recently I had some tapes put onto DVDs, and one of the items were some TV reports when I first took over the Black Caps. On one of those tapes was a very fresh-faced Nathan Astle, and the question asked of him at the time was, 'You've had one of the legends of New Zealand cricket in Glenn Turner be replaced by an Aussie. How do you think that will go?'

Nathan replied, 'Well, I don't know him yet, and I don't know much about him. We'll have to put up with him, won't we?'

These were his first words about me, which was interesting as the three years unwound. The Nathan I got to know was a very quiet, unassuming person, a very honest person, a person you don't try to belt things into, because it's not in his nature to respond well to that treatment. It's a softly-softly approach with coaching Nathan.

But if you win his confidence, you'll get the player we've all experienced, and it wasn't too long before I sat back and said to him, 'Well mate, if you're not the leading scorer of hundreds for New Zealand in one-day games, and maybe even in test matches, I'll be very surprised'.

And that was ahead even of the great Martin Crowe, who is a world great, not just in New Zealand.

I said to him, 'You'll have your share of doubts, but at the end of the day you'll be a major contributor'. He started to believe in that, and believe in me, and we built a very special relationship. We still stay in contact these days.

He can be stubborn if he doesn't believe in the message he's being given. I admire that. As a coach I don't like a person just standing there and accepting every word I say. I need to be challenged, and if I feel I'm barking up the wrong tree I will put up my hand and say I'm wrong.

With Nathan I could take on an approach with plan A, and if that didn't work go to plan B, and if that didn't work then plan C might work, and get the same result I was aiming for in the first place. If you present it right, and he understands it, it'll be fine. Understanding is the key. To sit there and talk about a major technique change wasn't the way to approach him. I had to get to understand the culture, the New Zealand way. I wasn't overly keen to do that originally, in the first three to four months. John Graham was very good in his assessment. He said to me, 'I think you need to understand how the Kiwis think'. I said, 'But I don't agree with some of the thinking, the negativity of how you play the game'. He said, 'Fine, but understand the culture'. So I sat back and took that good advice. I began to see the insecurities that needed to be amended. So I had to become a bit more delicate in the way I approached things. In the end I do believe there have been some changes in the Black Caps culture, a bit more flair, a bit more exuberance in the way they play the game. That's a reflection of that era.

I couldn't be prouder of the change, and Nathan was a major contributor to that change. I look now at players like Lou Vincent, Ross Taylor and Peter Fulton, and think that how they play is part of the legacy that Nathan's left — and that I had a part in shaping. That's what the game is really all about to me, and New Zealand can hopefully keep it going for a long time.

I was born and bred on the attitude that you didn't hold back on your opinion on what others in the team were doing. That was something I had to hold back on with such a young side. But once players like Nathan, Flem and Chris Cairns came on board with it, it was outstanding. That was the culture they built for the future.

Nathan was so important to the whole process, because he was the quiet achiever. Nobody would ever expect him to say anything at a team meeting, but when he did, everyone would just go, 'Shit, where did that come from?' and take notice. It was terrific for the team.

He's a free-flowing batsman who, on his day, can do some remarkable things. You have to understand you'll get some bad with the good, and once we sat down and he understood that I'd live with the bad, because the good would probably lead us to a couple of test victories, or one-day victories, he started to feel more comfortable with his own game. He knew where he stood with me, because I'd say to him, 'If you get out doing this, I can live with it, because on a different day that approach is going to win us a game'.

Let me give an example. We were in Australia in 1997–98, about to play a one-day game in Adelaide. I sat down with Nath, and said, 'Mate, as an opening bat, how are you going to approach [Glenn] McGrath?'. He said, 'I'm probably going to try to see him off'. I said, 'Mate, if you try to see him off, I'll tell you right now that over the one-day series, he's going to win the battle 95 per cent of the time, because that is what he wants people to do.

'What about taking him on? You know where the ball's going to be pitched, because he pitches the ball in the same spot every time. Nobody has ever approached him in an aggressive manner, which I think would lead to him having to change his line of attack. That's the sort of thing you must approach a bowler with. I want to see you going for none for 50 off eight overs.'

He said, 'Well how are we going to do that?'.

I said, 'You know where he's going to bowl it. So why don't we try going down the wicket to him. You've got all the blokes up, and if you're caught trying to play this style of game, I won't mind. Because if you let him dictate, he's going to beat us.'

Nathan was up for it. He said, 'Yeah, I'd like to do that, because you're right, if he gets it right enough times, he probably will nick me out'.

So Nathan went out, and he hit McGrath straight back over his head for six in the second over Glenn bowled, and Glenn looked shocked. He had that 'What the hell is going on here?' look on his face.

That day Glenn went for one for 53, Nathan made 66, and we set a target of 260 for seven, which won you a lot of games back then. Nathan had been asked to play a role and he did it perfectly.

Now we didn't win the game, but we made arguably the best team they were ever going to face work really hard. Mark Waugh got a terrific century, and Australia only had two balls to spare for the win. But it was more about the attitude of Nathan, and that approach would work for us many times.

Nathan's whole game was up there with the best. The reality with his fielding was that it was as good as it got. Our slip fielding then was extraordinary, and Nathan was a major contributor there.

When Stumper went back to Australia, my former Canterbury coach David Trist became the national coach. Tristy was extraordinarily enthusiastic, as he is in life, in all things really. Unless you've been around him, he's a hard man to explain. The nearest I could come is to say that's he's a living, breathing example of someone who is genuinely high on life.

No matter what sort of day you were having, you could rely on Tristy to pick you up, whether it was with a great story he had of his playing days, or his time coaching in Holland or South Africa, or just a cricket story in general. He had the knack of saying the right thing at the right time, of just making you feel good. If your self-belief, or feeling for the game, was slipping, he was the perfect man to bring it all back. If you needed advice on any technical aspect, and you went to him, once again he was able to read exactly what the situation called for.

Now, he's a great talker. He could happily talk with you for hours on end. But as well as knowing what to say if you were struggling with something, he also knew how much to say, without going too far, or carrying on until the message was lost.

What I loved about playing for the guy was that he made it fun to play for New Zealand. He always believed in the side, no matter what the situation was. His mood never seemed to change, which made it very easy to approach him.

That consistency was a huge thing, especially when you were touring. Most of us go through some mood swings on a long tour. I know that I did. At times I didn't want to be around anyone, I just wanted my own space, and didn't really want to talk to anyone at all. As much as you tried not to bring that into the team environment, sometimes it was hard not to.

But with Tristy that was never the case. If he was ever in a bad mood, or upset about something that had happened, you'd never have known it. He was constantly positive the whole way through.

David Trist (New Zealand coach 1999–2001): Nathan appears to be a very pragmatic type, who takes it as he sees it, plays it as he feels comfortable. He never required huge amounts of re-education in terms of how to go about it, and he wasn't a great one for practising, but had great natural ball-handling skills which he put to excellent use.

A very even character who didn't show great emotion, either out there, or once he was dismissed. It was very, 'Okay, I'm out'. That was it. So for him, his natural instincts, emotionally, psychologically, and physically, were ideal for playing the game of cricket the way he did.

He never tried to absorb the modern theories that were being pushed out, especially during my early days. There were a lot of ideas being canvassed, and he went along with it, but not to the degree that it affected his way of doing things. In a way, that was very interesting, because you have to say that the statistics prove that it worked for him. It may not have worked for other players, but I'm sure the other coaches gave him pretty much licence to be himself, recognising the individual differences in players.

Don't put too much into his head, because if you do, you're going to confuse him, and if you confuse him he won't play well, and he won't enjoy it. And he did play to get pleasure out of the actual game, not as a commercial interest.

When you have the outstanding eye-hand combination, and very fast hands that Nathan has, and look at the time when he opened for me, and then for Denis Aberhart, you can see that he scored most of his centuries for New Zealand during that period. It was a time where it was probably less complicated, and he had come through the early, bedding-down stages.

He was mature enough mentally to be able to say, 'Listen, I'm not going to take on board that gobbledygook, because it might work for him and him, but it's not going to work for me'. He would never challenge it, he would just go on and do it the way he did best.

For example, he never said a great deal at team meetings. There were debriefs after every day's play, and that can get extremely boring, trying to make them different. But when he did speak, people listened, and it was generally along the lines of, 'Come on, let's come down a little bit, and let's keep it simple'. It was usually quite pertinent.

When we played in the New Zealand team, we could lose three wickets in the first 15 overs, that was sort of the acceptable limit. Once, against Australia, we got it out to 100 runs in the first 15. I think Nathan enjoyed that attitude. He was much more dynamic as a player than he was as a person, and cricket is a sport that can allow you to express yourself in a way that you may not be able to away from the game.

I put the enjoyment he got from cricket down to him

having it uncomplicated, and I think that could work for more players. It always seemed to me that he understood what he could do, and what he couldn't do. At what point he reached that near nirvana, I'm not sure, but how he got there, I would have thought, was from his own experience.

Nathan developed shots that were played very late, intuitively, like the pull shot, where he would lift his front foot out of the way, and clear it, so he could pull the ball or hook the ball, which is a very, very technically good way of doing it. Very few people had done that before, and he just did it naturally. I don't believe he studied it, but he would often play almost a pull shot off the front foot, but with the front leg out of the way to clear the room to play through the off side.

On the off side he often didn't get right across to the ball, but he did generally get a very good plant, and then with his good eye and fast hands he hit through the line of the ball. So when you've got core stability, and a very good eye, your chances of cutting, which is one of his really powerful shots, or driving into the areas you wanted to, were quite high.

From a purist's point of view, he probably didn't have his head absolutely over the ball. He may have come down the wicket, seen it go wider, and just let the hands follow, which, with the wonderful eye-hand co-ordination he had, he could do.

He developed certain areas where he hit particularly well, and he also had a momentum to his game, which was not always conventional. He just trusted himself to hit the ball.

It's a little bit like the play you see in the modern game now that's being developed through Twenty20. There are a lot more non-cricket shots that are being developed; you can't define a particular shot as an on drive or a sweep, it's just the ball being hit away very effectively.

He had this wonderful ability to adapt and play shots that were often just outside the norm. For example, you'd often see him jumping as he played a shot on defence; he'd be off the ground, and that's seen as not being ideal. But because he was short, and had that wonderful elasticity in his body, it helped him get over the ball, and it worked for him. That tells you that there were things not absolutely perfect about his technique, but he scored runs, and he scored runs quickly.

You had to be careful not to try to change too much of his defensive game because he would, perhaps, lose the rhythm of his game, and his effectiveness. At times he would nick and be out, but everyone does that when you've got a new ball to deal with, as he often did.

Most of the down times he had were a result, I believe, of what was going on in his head, not technique. Disappointment at not getting runs would implode on him. As long as he trusted himself the record shows he would find form.

We talked about some things he did, but it was never in a 'must do' situation. 'Here are some things, how do you feel about them, think about it and come back.' That was pretty much all I did. I have no memory of him ever coming to me asking for assistance. He may have done it with players, which I always felt was a very good method. If he trusted a player, I didn't mind who he went to, Martin Crowe, whoever, it didn't matter to me. But I don't think he ever came to me about a really specific technical problem.

He refined his game, tightened it, and understood that he had to mix defence with attack. He gained a better perception of how he had to rotate the strike, and get singles, and not only look for the more expansive shots. That was only what you'd expect maturation to do. He showed enough sporting nous to understand those things and apply them pretty consistently right through.

Players found it easy to talk with Nathan because he was non-threatening, and, from my perception, everyone was equal in his eyes. If he thought that someone was coming to him to ask his opinion, he would respect the fact that he was being sought out for his knowledge. He never pontificated, and that's very helpful to other sportsmen, because a lot of people find it very challenging to ask for help. Some would see it as acknowledgement of a potential weakness.

I think he was always comforting for young players to be around, without actually doing much. He never threatened them, he never shouted at them, he never showed ill-discipline towards their psychological state. It's a very strong part of his makeup. He very rarely showed disappointment in their performances.

His strength would be talking to younger players one-on-one, telling them how he went about it, what he gained from his experiences, and letting them see that there is another way of doing it. It doesn't have to be as it was in the past.

In the last 20 years, like rugby, cricket has changed significantly, and the coaching methodology has changed hugely, so the hymn sheet is being sung at different levels with the different types of the game.

I was pretty easy with him. I don't think I ever challenged him on anything. But most of the time, when he went out to bat he switched into another gear, and he really was, within his own mind, wanting to do the best he could, and was always, always, trying. Nathan and Stephen Fleming had an inner burn that you sometimes don't get from people with a more nurtured background.

But Nathan was never a player — as some are — who lives on emotions that can destabilise their form. The only time I can remember Nathan showing, I suppose you'd call it disappointment, maybe resentment, was when we'd come back from South Africa at the end of 2000. It was a very challenging time. We had to regroup. I had indicated to New Zealand Cricket that I didn't want to proceed with my contract.

We were playing Zimbabwe, who at that time were a competitive unit. They had all their top players, the Flowers, Heath Streak. Richard Hadlee came out in a paper saying that some of the top players really had to step up to the plate. Nathan and Craig McMillan were singled out, and they both got hundreds [Astle 142, McMillan 141], and it felt very much as if they really wanted to get centuries.

There was a cartoon in the Wellington paper that showed Nathan and Craig standing like schoolboys, with Richard saying, 'I told you so', or something like that. I put it up in the dressing room, and Macca came up and said, 'What the **** is this?' and tore it up. Nathan just smiled, but I think he agreed with Macca.

When I was coach with the New Zealand side my wife Christine travelled with me, which was part of the contract. I don't believe the players found her threatening, and she isn't. We were in India in 1999, where Nathan did very well, topping our one-day batting averages, and we played pretty good cricket, even though we lost the test series and lost the one-day series.

Each city that we came to Christine would go and look through the *Lonely Planet* and we'd put together a two-page newsletter, and our manager Jeff Crowe would always arrange a bus. We'd say, if you want to go to see a palace, we leave at such and such a time. Very few embraced the culture and the idea of discovery. Some of them did, but they were still quite young, and they possibly have done more since. It was very much part of my feeling that we have to be expanded as people to understand the beauty and the joy of the game. It's not just cricket, there's life out there.

Nathan generally was less enamoured with such things. He didn't see them as frivolous, but he was much happier on a golf course. He was happier with a lifestyle that surrounded him with sport.

In South Africa, Jeff and I put together what we called a captain's club, where six players would be our guests and we'd pick the menu and the wine, because those were things that interested us. Nathan would go, but it wasn't something he really embraced. I didn't have any problem if Nathan hadn't embraced that, because it's just not some people's go. He enjoyed what he enjoyed, and didn't expand a great deal outside that.

He was always a balanced sort of guy, wasn't a womaniser, enjoyed himself, but kept a handle on it. What you see is what you get. He was self-contained, he never created unhappiness within the team and never talked himself up.

I have a tremendous amount of respect for Denis Aberhart. He was a coach whose great skill was in the way he handled people. He knew how guys worked. He knew exactly what to say if you were struggling, at just the right time. To me, he was underrated as a New Zealand coach, maybe because he was a low-key sort of guy who wasn't going to make statements that would go straight into the headlines.

There weren't a lot of accolades during his time as national coach, which was very unfair, because his win-to-loss ratio in tests (75%) was far better than Stumper's (60%), Tristy's (41%), or Brace's (43%).

When you added one-day games, the overall win-to-loss ratio goes: Braces, 52%, Denis, 52%, Stumper, 43%, and Tristy, 40%.

The results speak for themselves really. It's my belief that Flem was at his best when he was working with Denis, where he was able to be his own man and work in partnership with the coach, not under his specific direction.

Denis Aberhart (New Zealand coach 2001–2004): I think Nathan went through periods when he did try to adjust his footwork, but his strength is hand-eye co-ordination, his ability to see the ball late, and play it late.

The only thing I ever said to Nathan was that he had a wee movement that was a bit late. Sometimes the old hand-eye co-ordination would not be quite enough. You needed to encourage him, of course, like any player. If he was going through one of his little bad phases, which could happen with the way he plays, it's just a matter of encouragement.

We'd talk sometimes if he'd had a bad run, and he'd think about changing things. I'd ask, 'Why?' and say, 'You do what you like, but you're going to come back to what you did before anyway. It's your head that's wrong; when that's right the runs will come again.'

He played from the crease, stood up tall, and sometimes he got out early playing a little bit square on the off side. But his record speaks for itself. He had a technique that allowed him to perform at the best levels. People would look at Nathan and say, 'He's a bit laid back; he's a bit horizontal'. But inside that was a guy who knew how he wanted to play, was comfortable with how he played, and once he got in, well, we saw the 16 one-day hundreds, the next highest tally before that [by a New Zealander] was four.

I think he was very good technically. He had the tools

to do the job, and the only time he wasn't so effective was when his confidence was down. There was no need for him to change in any great way. You would see Nathan charge a fast bowler. He hit guys straight so well that he could charge down the wicket and hit them. When he was on song, he never missed. And he still had time to bail out. That was the strength of his game; he had the ability to go down the track at the bowler, and most times he'd nail it, but if he didn't, he had time to bail out, which is a real ability, a real skill.

You would see him batting, and then all of a sudden he'd take off. People would say, 'Nathan gets a flyer at the start of his innings'. But a lot of his hundreds would come up in the 40th over or so. So there was the ability to give it the fly, but also the ability to take responsibility, carry on, and finish the job. There are a lot of players who couldn't finish the job. Most times, especially in his early career, if he got 50, he got 100. His ability to convert was great.

There would be periods in his innings when he'd be quiet, and then he'd explode like a firecracker. To me, that showed a mental toughness that people at times might not have thought he had. So there was steely resolve under that relaxed demeanour, quite focused on what he wanted to achieve.

He had good game skills, whether it was soccer or cricket. He knew what had to be done, knew strategies. He had good natural fitness, and he had good ball skills. So he was always someone who was going to be successful.

In a very quiet, laid-back way he knew what was needed for him to get ready for matches. At times he would get frustrated by people telling him what he needed to do. Hell, *he already knew*. If he wasn't very happy about something, he would let you know, not involving anyone else, just quietly getting his point over.

He isn't shy, he's just quiet. He went about doing his job, enjoyed it, and enjoyed other people's successes as well. No big ego, so he had no problem with other people having the limelight — in fact it actually suited him. (Laughs.) He could keep his head down. Basically, he's a good bloke, a good team man, all those things.

In a team, Nathan was never comfortable to get up and make a speech to rally the guys, but in the background, talking to new guys, supporting guys who were out of form, welcoming new guys, he could do the whole gamut. He was a ready ear, he would always listen, and the players quickly learned he was not judgemental. So therefore they were able to talk to him; and in his own quiet way, while he wouldn't search them out, he would be there for them.

He's got a keen, dry sense of humour, enjoys interacting with people; he could be your brother, and that's what makes teams click often, not the people at the front, but the people who are quite happy to sit round, listen to people, chew the fat. There was no one that he couldn't interact with.

Gary Stead: Nathan was there in my first test match [in Christchurch against South Africa in 1999] when I went in at No. 5. He came down after the first over, and said, 'Aw, this is just like the old Shirley Boys' High days'.

It was something that was quite comforting in a way. He had that calming influence on people. He always had very simple messages, such as 'Keep going'; 'See you again soon'; 'What's happening?'; and 'Just watch the ball'.

I never saw him rattled. He just went about it in his own way. He never seemed rushed, even when he was out of form. He will say that that's when things speed up, but he never relayed that to us when we were playing alongside him.

Geoff Allott: I think in the first half of his career he soaked it all up, what was going on around him. Then, when new guys came into the side, he had the ability to read a player's situation, and almost judge and assess whether that was detrimental or advantageous to the player's own performance.

I remember one particular occasion when we were on the way to the Commonwealth Games in 1998, and we were at a tournament in Singapore. We were playing Pakistan, I think. On the bus, I was trying to psyche myself up on the way to the game, the way I was used to from rugby days. Nathan was sitting beside me just cracking up with laughter. It pierced my concentration, and made me realise that I was getting too tense.

His own method was probably a bit too relaxed for me, but a happy medium was what he'd identified for me, not even by actually coming out and saying it directly, but with the great knack he had of alluding to it. He was almost the silent assassin in a way. He was not someone renowned for being vocal in the team meetings, but with the respect he had in the team, he could just hint at something that could be useful and you took note of it.

At team meetings when Nath spoke, everyone always took notice. When something meant enough for him to speak out, that meant it needed serious attention. It was his strength, especially in his later years, that he must have recognised how much people did respect him, so he offered more, which is tremendous for the team.

Denis Aberhart: He was a very loyal person if you were a coach. He was supportive, and you knew that if he had something he needed to discuss he'd come to you, it would never be behind your back. He wasn't ever high maintenance.

Someone who you could sit down, have a good chat with, and say, 'What do you reckon?'. Nathan is a very structured person, and he knew exactly what he needed to do to play. How much he needed, how to go about it, how much work. It was all straightforward stuff, but he always had a plan and he stuck to it.

You could call it simple, but I'd call it structured, I'd call it knowing, and that was him. That's why he wasn't high maintenance. He was an easy tourist, happy with what he was doing, didn't need anything elaborate when he was travelling.

When I was first in the New Zealand team I found life on the road great. I enjoyed living out of a suitcase, seeing new places, never having to cook a meal, getting organised at every new hotel. Although, when we went to countries like India and Pakistan it was different, because the attention on players there is so intense.

Cricket is such a massive sport there. Whenever you went outside, people wanted to talk to you, to be around you. Coming home from tours like that I'd be at a stage where I really wanted to have my own space, to stay at home by myself, to watch my own television. Some days I almost couldn't be bothered to talk to anyone.

Looking back, it irks me that I let it get to me, to the point of drawing back from even my own family, who had done so much over the years. Then, when Kelly and I were together, she didn't have to stay behind all the time, but instead was often able to travel and stay with me. The New Zealand management had a sensible attitude, I thought. They knew that the demands on us to be away from home were so great, that the effect on relationships could be devastating if our partners weren't able to see us.

In recent years we've all had our own room at hotels, so that made it a lot easier for your wife to join you on the road. In my life, the big change came when our children were born, and started to grow up. Kelly wasn't able to travel on many occasions, and I started to feel real homesickness for probably the first time in my life.

Geoff Allott: To say that Nathan is one of the most tidy people in the history of the world is possibly an understatement. (Laughs.) It's bordering on an obsession. I remember looking in the cupboard of the house he shared with Flem, and I honestly couldn't believe it.

There were all his shoes, at least 12 pairs, lined up on two racks. They were in groups, the formal ones, the casual pairs. All his shirts went in order, whether they were short-sleeved, long-sleeved, what colour they were, all of them ironed, and of course, matching jackets. I understand that when he was living with Flem they hired a woman just to iron Nathan's shirts.

On tour, where you'd think that'd fall away, Nathan would unpack for 90 minutes, find the right coat hangers, put his shirts away and organise all his clothes. Without question he was the tidiest tourist, by quite a long way, in the Black Caps.

I'd have to say he was a very stylish dresser, too, and with generous sponsors as well, it'd be fair to say that he never went short of clothes to wear.

John Astle: One advantage Nathan always had when he travelled was that he was tidy. He would never have had to scoop things up, and try to find things, and pile things in. When he was in age teams I remember coaches using him as an example of how they should be ready and organised. He's never been a great collector, of souvenirs and photographs. A lot of people do, but he doesn't do that at all.

Lee Astle: He always had everything organised. He had a place for everything. Nathan could pack and be ready to go to England in half an hour, and nothing would be missing.

Denis Aberhart: Nathan always wanted to do well, to succeed. He felt he had the recipe, and when you look back, I think he did have the recipe. He could get frustrated sometimes with being offered technical advice, and there are people in New Zealand cricket who would try to give it to him. Basically, the guy had played a lot of cricket, and things had gone okay for him. Yes, there were things that he might have changed, but would they have made him a better player? I don't know. They might have made him look better, but whether they would have actually made him a more effective player I'm not sure.

His knees were a bit crook towards the end of his career, so he couldn't bowl as much, which frustrated him, because he enjoyed his bowling. He bowled so straight, and did just enough with the ball. Around the world he was feared for what he could do in a game, how he could change the course of a match.

He could play in more than just one way, like the test in Auckland where he batted with Danny Morrison for a record last wicket stand in 1997, and then down here at Jade Stadium where he decided to get a couple of hundred fairly quickly.

In New Zealand terms there's no one close, and in the late 1990s, and the early 2000s, I don't believe there were many in the whole world with better all-round performances.

As a fielder he had very, very good hands, and he was much better in the outfield than people gave him credit for. He covered the ground reasonably well, and his pick-up and throw was very quick. If I were picking a team of players who were going to perform for me, of all the players I've coached, he'd be in the side. And if I were going to pick a team of bloody good blokes, a good team man, he'd be in the side too.

He'd be one of the first blokes I'd pick for both teams, and a lot of players wouldn't be in both teams.

You could say that Nathan was quite happy to be a blue-collar worker, while some of our players are white-collar workers. He crossed over between the two beautifully, and was well respected by both groups.

Geoff Allott: As a batsman, Nathan was brutal on the front foot and on width, against any attack. If you erred, you paid for it, and he would only need one or two good shots to be away. Especially in one-day cricket, where you have early fielding restrictions, you could normally bowl back of a length and angling across, but Nath would punish you.

So the only place to bowl to him, as a left-armer, was to bowl around the wicket and try to bowl at his chest. That was fine if the wicket had a bit of pace and could bounce pretty steeply. But the majority of wickets were fairly well paced, and Nathan developed the ability to hit square. Even though it wasn't a full-blooded hook shot, with his timing and his strength, if he got onto it, he hit a six.

I consider his timing to have been the best of anyone I played with, and he had a great knack of getting very good pieces of willow, often about six inches thick on the edges. I think he was one of the first players in the New Zealand side to get such bats, and, as we all know, when he hit it, it stayed hit.

His bats weren't heavier than a normal bat. Kookaburra

worked with him to produce a bat that I believe was a lot thicker on the sides. It was more wood, but it was lighter wood, it wasn't pressed as hard. So the bats might not have lasted as long, but they were lighter, and had a bigger sweet spot. I was fortunate to be given a couple of them as hand-me-downs, not that I ever had much of a chance to use them, but the bats were tremendous.

It's all credit to Nath, because he stayed within the laws of the game, but he looked for a change that gave him some advantage. And he found something that worked for him. In a way it was typical of him, that he had a simple change, and he had the ability to make the change, where other players mainly stuck with the status quo.

I don't think it's an overstatement to say that he's been one player, certainly in New Zealand, who has really influenced the way the one-day game has been played — in particular, in the way the first 15 overs are used.

The way he played, unless you had the hand-eye co-ordination and strength he had, it was almost impossible to appreciate what he was achieving. In the early stages, it wasn't readily recognised as a way to play the game. I think people came to realise that he's not a flamboyant sort of person, but inwardly he knows when he's on song, he knows when things are going right; and when he drove square, or drove straight, or over the covers, in the early stages, he went about it with certainty, and the manner and the speed with which the ball was hit meant that, in a way, he created his own niche.

It was always very hard to read Nathan's body language, always difficult as a bowler to try to work out whether he was mentally tough or not, or even just to see how he was feeling on a particular day, and that was an advantage for him. Even if he wasn't in good nick, or wasn't feeling in good nick, because his emotive state changed very little when he was batting, people couldn't recognise it, pick up on it, and take advantage of it.

Along with Flem in the slips, I can only count two occasions when they ever dropped a catch. They were just outstanding. When you consider his disability with his thumb, it's not a bad effort. How that didn't get hit more often, I'll never know. His terrific fielding highlights the fact that any really special batsman is usually also a super fieldsman.

What shows how different their ability is from others, is how cleanly they can take the ball. They know precisely which direction it's coming from, the trajectory of the ball, versus hitting thumbs and wrists and forefingers. They middled them every time, and I think that's almost an indication that the only time he might ever drop a catch was when he was out of batting nick. But 99 per cent of the time they would stick. The other point I'd like to reiterate is that I've never thought that people have respected his bowling enough. It was always great to have him bowling from the other end. It probably gets forgotten because, later on in his career, his back injury limited how much he was able to bowl, but he had a great record as a bowler. His accuracy, discipline, use of the slower ball and ability to reverse swing it, was amazing.

But if you round out the picture on Nathan, looking at his batting ability, his ability to catch, and his bowling ability, he would be for me one of the two best players, along with Chris Cairns, that I ever played with.

My last coach for New Zealand was, of course, John Bracewell. John reads a lot of books about how to read people, how they tick, and I felt that he reached a stage where he thought he could tell what was going on inside a guy's head. So rather than going to a player and asking what was up, he'd make an assumption. There were times, I believe, when he got those assumptions wrong. It also seemed to me that when he took over, he took a long time to trust what he was told by the players. So rather than ask, and take the answer at face value, he seemed at times to prefer observation and assumption to what he'd been told.

For someone like me, the way I play my cricket, he was too complicated, there was too much going on. There was no clear path to what was happening around us. People were being left out, teams were changing, and people didn't know why it was happening. I think that sometimes John was so enthusiastic in his coaching that it could get away on him. He would have all these ideas running through his head, and he'd throw all of them at you at once. Obviously, some guys deal with that better than others. I was one that just thought, 'Jeez, take a step back man, just give me one idea at a time'.

He's that sort of guy. I think he means well, but for me he was a bit too complicated. When I look back, other coaches seem to have read me, and knew how I worked. Don't get me wrong, John wants players to do well as much as any coach I've ever had. But I feel he gets too wound up in what he's doing. I think that at times there's so much going on in John's head that he can head off on tangents, whereas what I'd be looking for from a coach is something specific and concise.

Glenn Turner: My assumptions were [when Nathan retired] that apart from feeling psychologically spent with the game, and asking himself why he was going out to play a game, and not coming up with a satisfactory answer, I wonder whether he started to lose a little bit of touch, and he wasn't playing as consistently as he did. And that may well be because his technique required such perfect timing. Only you can come to that realisation that you're not enjoying the game any more.

People can't understand why you want to give up. I guess the supporter would love to do what you do, and I guess a lot can't understand why you wouldn't want to keep doing it until you drop dead. (Laughs.)

David Trist: Lack of enjoyment can stem from a number of things. The team environment. The clear message from Ric Charlesworth was that players were going to be put under pressure. That didn't go down too well with Chris Cairns and it didn't work with Nathan. Those two should have been at the [2007] World Cup.

Did it work with other players in the team? I don't see the same fervour to play for the Black Caps as there is to play for the All Blacks. It's not as large a talent pool. Each individual has different switches that turn them on, and there are some who, if you threaten them, you're not going to win.

Denis Aberhart: Nathan'll be very much missed for his quiet contributions in the New Zealand side. He's never sought a profile, just gone about his job. Scored 11 test centuries and 16 one-day centuries. That says it all, really. To drop him so that he'd get the message was, I think, a mistake. It's not the way you get the best out of Nathan. You work alongside him.

Flem

Stephen Fleming is one of my closest friends, which is just as well, because we've spent a huge amount of time in each other's company. We'd been together in the Black Caps for nearly two years when he first captained the side in 1996, when he was only 23, which is very young to be leading an international side.

In the decade that followed I've watched him grow in the job, and the confidence he's got has come with experience. He handles it all very, very well. The pressures put on him as captain are pretty taxing on their own, and he's had to look after his other job of batting as well.

For a guy who is so highly rated by the likes of Richie Benaud and Ian Chappell, it's odd that he's often been bagged by our local television commentators. They often cite what they see as his lack of energy, lack of spark. Out on the field he's not a big demonstrative guy, and I know at times our television commentators have said, 'Fleming has to get more involved, he has to inject some emotion'.

His argument is that he's not there to run around like a headless chicken, and wear his heart on his sleeve. It's not him. When he's captaining a side in a test or a one-day game, there's so much going on, whether it's who is going to bowl next, who's bowled how many overs from what end, field placements, and what we can do to get out a batsman who's sticking around.

When you look around the world, there aren't many emotional-looking captains out there. Steve Waugh, Ricky Ponting, Flem, they're all pretty stern-looking characters when they're captaining their country. It's just part of being captain of an international side. Fans and critics need to realise there's a lot more you have to think about than what you see on television. I think he hides his emotions, not because he has to, but because there's a lot of other stuff he has to get right for his team to perform well. He does show emotion, in the shed, and when we get wickets, and when his batting goes well. I can say that in all the years we've known each other, we've only had one real argument, and that was when we were flatting together in a house we'd bought.

Stephen Fleming: Rather than just flatting in our early days in the New Zealand team we thought it'd be a good investment to put some money in and buy a property. We were trying to make some money out of the house, as well as flatting.

One of us did [make some money] and one of us didn't. Nathan had met Kelly, so he was moving on with his life. We got a valuation done, which we both thought was fair and I bought his share out. I held onto the house for another six months, and either the market turned considerably worse in those six months, or the valuation that Nathan organised was a touch over the top.

It's fraught with danger when you split a house. He made some good money out of it, and I lost a little bit. He's always seemed to have a golden touch with those sorts of moves, so I've always followed his investments closely.

While we've had the odd discussion when we haven't thought along the same lines as far as cricket goes, we've never had any real arguments. And when you look at how much time we've spent together, touring, flatting, on the cricket field, on the golf course, it is almost remarkable that we've never had a huge barney.

Well, not unless you count throwing chips at a mate as a barney. As I remember it, I'd been invited to a function, and at first said I'd go to it. I changed my mind, and he had to do it. That was when the chips flew.

Stephen Fleming: He can be so frustrating because he's so easy going, that he can agree to do things for people, things that I'd class as commitments. How it went was that I'd agree to tag along to a function just to help out, and meanwhile he'd arrange to do something else, and pull out. I'd still go.

It happened a few times, and I tried to tell him that when you make a commitment you should stick to it. He just wouldn't have it. He was out and about a bit at the time. It got to a stage where, one Friday night when we were going out, I wasn't happy about it and I lost my rag with him. It's the only time it ever happened.

It taught him commitment and he was much better after that. We were having Friday-night fish and chips, and they were the only thing close, so I grabbed a handful. He'd been chiding me in that subtle goading way as he was going up the hallway, so I grabbed a handful and he copped them in the back of the swede.

He's very unassuming on the surface, but underneath there's quite a wicked sense of humour. He can be very cutting with his remarks, but it's done without malice. While he's never come across as being sarcastic or nasty, there's a sense of humour that keeps people on edge, and continues to keep people on edge, which makes him reasonably interesting. Until you get to know him, of course, and then he's boring as hell. (Laughs.)

It's unexpected when a line pops up. If he were someone who was always having a go, teasing people, you'd expect it. But with Nathan it just pops out of nowhere, so it cuts a little bit deeper. (Laughs.)

He was always such an easy-going guy that when we finally played in the same team, he was someone you didn't mind spending a lot of time with, you just naturally gravitated towards him. It was a gradual thing. There was no sort of dawning when I suddenly thought, 'This bloke's alright'. Over time I just found that I enjoyed his company. As we grew, we often found ourselves the younger players in a team, so that also helped us to stick together. Obviously, I enjoyed the way he played cricket, and in a social sense there was no fuss, he was just a nice guy to be around.

Flem's always been a very elegant sort of player, which is often the case with left-handers. Some come to mind that aren't as fluent; Allan Border would be one. But guys like Flem and David Gower do look more elegant.

He's also a guy that maintains his composure, which isn't always easy. When the team's not doing so well, and you're not going so well with the bat, and you have to front the media after every game, it gets very taxing. I'm sure it affects him, but he's the sort of guy that, for the sake of the team, as a leader, keeps the stresses under wraps pretty well. Over the years, we have had chats about how at times it can be hard to get up every day when things aren't going well. But that's part and parcel of what he has to do.

If you listen to him when he gives interviews, he doesn't speak in clichés. He tells you what he's really feeling. Even in games where you're losing, he'll say what he thinks, and tell the public what we need to be working on and what's not going right.

Steve Rixon appointed him as the fulltime captain in 1997 to replace Lee Germon. Through the coaching eras of David Trist and Dennis Aberhart he had, in my opinion, pretty much the run of the team, and that's when I think he was at his best and playing his best cricket. Through that period I saw him get a lot stronger as a person and believe in himself a lot more. Now he handles everything that's thrown at him very well.

He's definitely grown into it, and now, as a captain, I don't think there are any better around the world.

Stephen Fleming: We already had a very strong relationship by the time we got into the New Zealand team. I remember the very first test when I was asked to be a caretaker captain, I went back to the house and said to Nath, 'What the hell do I do tomorrow?'.

We sat down and had a chat about it, so right from my first game as captain he had a pretty strong influence on what we did. But it was only when he was prompted. He wouldn't be too proactive about coming up with suggestions or ideas. He trusted what was going on.

When I asked for it, though, he had a pretty clear understanding about what needed to be done, and how it should be done. He was never overly forthcoming or overbearing, and that's what drew me to him. Especially when he was standing at second slip a lot of the time, we talked a lot about what was happening, and how the game was playing out.

So I had Nathan Astle on one side, and Adam Parore on the other side. You couldn't get two more differing personalities to get information from.

To me, when the captain walks over the line, he's got to be confident about the men he's got there with him. The coach is there to coach, and that's his job. But the captain has to believe in the guys on the field with him, and I believe that for that reason the captain should have a fair say in the selection of the team.

It's true that under John Bracewell, Flem didn't have the same involvement in all aspects of the team and its play as he'd had before. But I don't want to give the impression that he was pushed out of power. I think that he did want to lessen the load that he was carrying. I'm pretty sure it was something he wanted to do.

Captaining a cricket team is a different art from firing up a side that plays for a much shorter length of time, as in soccer or rugby. Every night before a game, we have a team meeting when the team gets named.

Before a test match we have a cap presentation. We have a past player, or someone who is held in high regard in the game in New Zealand. They'll talk about what the black cap meant to them, or, if it's someone else, their thoughts in general. Then they'll present the caps.

Then Flem will speak, and that's it. There may be a few words spoken before we go out onto the field, but there won't be a fire-and-brimstone, hand-smacking, roaring team talk.

How he goes about his leadership is that he gets on with everyone, but somehow also manages to keep a little bit aloof, as a captain has to. The captain is one of the boys, yet he's not one of the boys, and he's managed to keep that balance very well.

He's good mates with a lot of people in the team, but they also know that, as the captain, if he says something he's decided on, you know where you stand with him, and you accept it. It's a huge skill he has, that he has managed to develop over a number of years.

Very occasionally he'll give you the edge of his tongue. Not a lot, but if he feels it's warranted or needed, it'll definitely come out. I think he knows what's needed and when it's needed. He's a very good analyst, and in the last few years that's been important, as we've done a lot more scouting of the opposition. We'll sit down with the technology that's available now, and try to pick out weaknesses in a player. I'm sure they do the same to us.

Before a game, Flem will have meetings with the bowlers. He's the sort of guy that will give the bowlers ideas, but not until they've outlined their plan. He wants to get their thoughts, know what they're thinking, and then he'll try to marry the two up. He's not the sort of guy who'll say, 'This is how you're going to bowl'. I think that's another positive with his captaincy. He makes each player think. You can't just turn up and expect him to have everything done for you. You have to have your own plans. It's the same with batting. You've got to have your game plan that you think is right with the game situation.

The bowlers will sit down with Flem, going through things before the game, and then, on the day, if he thinks it's needed, he'll go to the bowler with his thoughts. He will always have a reason why he wants something done. You might not agree with it, but out there he's the captain, and you have to trust his judgement.

He may talk to me, or one or two other senior players, before he goes to a bowler, just to sound out his ideas, but then, when he goes to a bowler with an idea, he'll believe in it, and he'll always have a reason why. He would never go to someone and say, 'You've got to do this now', and then walk away.

I can't speak highly enough of how, as a captain, he approaches players and talks things through with them. We'll all have disagreements, but you have to be big enough to know that he is your captain and sometimes you just have to do what he's asking you to do. After all, the success or failure of the team does fall back mainly on his head. He's the one facing the heat from the media at the end of play.

He can think outside the square, and because things have worked, he's gained a lot of confidence. His gut feelings are usually on the money, or pretty close to it. He reads the game, as a good captain does in any sport, whether it's cricket, rugby, or soccer. They tend to have a good feel for it, and Flem certainly has that, which allows him to do those odd little off-the-wall things that have worked for us over the years.

We play a lot of golf together. For me, when we're away on tour you have that many meetings and training sessions, that many commitments, that sometimes it's just good to get away and lose yourself on a golf course. I've found, over the years, that when I've been struggling for form — when you tend to worry more and train more — you can get tense, and to go out and play a round of golf, and just forget everything, gives me a mental break that refreshes me. Flem, Scotty Styris, Brendon McCullum and I always enjoy doing it.

The golden time for the golfers was when Jeff Crowe was the manager. Jeff loved his golf, and, as someone who had taken golfing tours around the world, he had a lot of great contacts. You've got to have your release, and whether it's doing that, or going to the movies or shopping, as some guys do, it's important to have it. It's the same as any job, if you do it 24/7 it's going to take its toll.

In general, we didn't talk about cricket when we were playing golf. Although sometimes it was talked about in a more casual way, away from a formal team situation. I think that Flem — and he might disagree with me — if he did talk about cricket when he was out playing golf, he was usually just trying to get a few ideas out of you in a less formal environment. I'm sure he took some things on board. But generally, the golf was pure relaxation, you got away, and tried to take each other's money.

At other times, in other places, we sometimes had strong discussions over cricket, and there were occasions when we'd walk away, neither one agreeing with the other. We'd hammer it out, and it was obvious our biggest difference was that while I do think about the game, I like to keep it as simple as I can, and he often had other ideas.

One thing we learned through Steve Rixon, is that the Aussie way is to get things out in the open, on the table. Not everyone is going to agree. That's life. The biggest thing is that you can't hold a grudge, because in a team people all work differently.

Sometimes someone will say something that gets you a bit fired off, and then you think, 'Hang on, maybe he has hit on something here, because it's annoyed me'. Even if it's one out of three that hits the mark, you're learning things as you go. I'd like to think that he's learned things from me. I've certainly learnt from him.

Stephen Fleming: Telling people things they don't really want to hear, especially those you're very good friends with, can be very difficult, but Nathan and I always had a very honest relationship, and we were able to talk from a very early age about the game, and how to succeed at it, so that all helped. So did his nature. He's not one to get all defensive if you tell him something he doesn't agree with. He'll tell you he doesn't agree with it, but that'll be the end of it. He's an easy guy to talk and deal with and that's probably why our relationship was so strong.

When you spend so much time together, it's important not to let things fester. If it does, eventually the shit's going to hit the fan, and someone will cop it at the completely wrong time. It's much better, if something is annoying you, to go to that person, and say, 'Look, I don't agree with this', or 'I think this is wrong'. Getting it off your chest is a big, good thing that Steve Rixon brought to the team.

That's the environment I enjoyed the most when I was playing. I'm not a confrontational sort of person, but if a thing is annoying me, then saying something about it was what we were encouraged to do. We had people like Cairnsy and Dion Nash, who would say what they thought, whether you liked it or not. You needed to take a step back, and realise they were doing it for the betterment of the team, or you as a player. If you disagreed with what they were saying then usually there was something behind it, and they'd hit a nerve, and they were right.

Stephen Fleming: Nathan has a very good cricket brain, and in some ways he probably didn't make the most of that. He tended to sit back and go with the flow, not wanting to be too much of a decision-maker. It was really only in the last couple of years, when he was pushed and prodded a lot, that he started to come forward more.

The quality he did bring was that if he did say something, people would always listen. Often, with the silent type, that can work well. Some of the most successful people I know sit back, listen, take it all in, and then what they give you is precise, to the point, and they suggest you get on with it.

I've often questioned myself as to whether, if we pushed too much, we would lose that leadership aspect he does bring. He had a very good relationship with everybody in the team, from myself to the most junior player in the side, and that's leadership in itself.

As a batsman there were two, or maybe three phases that Nathan went through. There was the phase where he was in great form, when he'd see the ball and hit it. There was the second phase where he would see the ball, but if it wouldn't come off, he'd get out. That led to the lack of form phase, which was incredibly interesting to be around. Nathan would go from being a very straightforward player, to one who would start searching for the technical side of things.

He was like a fish out of water when he was in that phase. I'd be trying to give him information, and I suppose complicate the game for him, in an attempt to help him get out of that phase himself without searching too hard.

I'm almost the exact opposite. I'm very technical in the way I look at the batting side and the way I'm playing, whereas he is very much a feel player and a form player. Somewhere in the middle I tried to get a blend for both of us. I know it pissed Nathan off at times when I'd try to hit him with too much technical stuff, but in the end he would have to come to it to try to snap himself out of the form slump he saw himself in.

But looking at it, that was probably part of the problem. If he just relaxed and trusted his usual style, he would have probably bounced back into form a lot quicker than the gathering information and going through the nets scenarios that he did.

The quality of athlete that he was, he was very much a hand-eye co-ordination guy who within the space of three or four shots could be in or out of form. One thing I'm not sure about is whether coaches and players let him play that certain way because it was deemed the way to get the best out of him. I always thought he had a little bit more to give. If he'd had a bit more technical nous he could have been a more consistent player. The good days would have still been good. The bad days would have been okay, rather than having big up and downs.

That'd be where we probably differed on our approaches to the game. In the end, it felt like I was pushing him too much, and he told me at times that I was. So we agreed to differ on some technical aspects of the game.

Flem's always presented well in public, one of those people who on most occasions looks like he's just stepped out of the shower. I'm not saying that he's a different man behind the scenes, but in the tidiness stakes the guys in the team know the truth. On tour they jibe me about my room and how everything is nicely folded or in the drawers. If you looked in Flem's room there's gear all over the show. Not a lot, to be fair to him, but it is usually spread out. He's impeccable in his presentation when he goes out. But behind the scenes, he's not quite as spotless as he looks.

Memories of Mates

Shane Bond and I have known each other for a long time: I went to his 21st birthday party. As time went by, after that, we didn't see so much of each other. I was playing for New Zealand, so away a lot, and he went into the police force.

Then, one year, all of a sudden, he was playing cricket again. He'd had a few stress fractures earlier on, so he decided to get a career behind him in the police. When he came back to Christchurch, at the end of 2000, everyone was talking about how quick he was bowling. He'd got a lot stronger after his time in the police, and that extra strength paid off for him.

When he went into the New Zealand side, his first test was against Australia in Hobart, and the first wicket he took was Steve Waugh, out lbw for a duck. Not a bad wicket to start your test career with. And it was nice to have someone in our side who was genuinely quick — quick enough to worry the Australians.

Bondy's a guy who tells it as it is. You know where you stand with him, which I think is a very good thing. If there's something on his mind, he'll tell it to your face, and then move on, which is something I applaud.

He is someone who cops a roasting from angry talkback callers because of his injuries. There have even been suggestions that he gets injured so often because he doesn't keep himself fit enough, or doesn't train enough. The truth is almost the complete opposite. He's one of the hardest workers I've ever seen in the team.

I saw that at close range. When I had a knee operation in 2003, he had another stress fracture, so we did a lot of work together in the gym. What people don't fully understand with a genuine fast bowler is the stress he puts his body under. At the pace I bowl, I can't explain it, or fully appreciate it. But to get up, day in, day out, and go back out and put that huge stress on your body . . . Such a huge amount of your body weight slams down on your leading leg when you bowl. By its very nature, fast bowling is going to see a player injured more easily than others.

He's had three or four stress fractures in his spine over his career. To be mentally strong enough to want to get back after that, to want to do the work, and keep playing to the level he's got to, is extra-ordinary. It's easy for people to sit back and say, 'Aw, he's injured, he's not tough enough, he should give it away'. But if they followed him around for two or three months, to see what he puts into the game behind the scenes, they'd surely have to eat their words.

A stress fracture isn't some figment of the imagination. It shows up on scans and X-rays. It's as real as a bone snapping in half. If you've ever had a really sore back you'll know how painful it can be. So to get out and bowl, to keep giving it a crack, with steel pins in his back, is a measure of how mentally tough Bondy is.

I'm sure that a lot of players, after two or three stress fractures, would have said, 'No, I've had enough of this'. But that's not Shane; he's come back, and is a vital member of the Black Caps. In one-day internationals he's taken 125 wickets at an average of just 19.32, and his economy rate is 4.20 per over, and that's phenomenal really. How could you criticise a man with averages like that?

He's developed his control and his variation too. He knows his game inside out. I'd call Bondy 'street smart'. As he's got older, he's matured a great deal, whether from his time in the police force, or the fitness battles he's had. He also thinks a lot about the game of cricket, and not only has a range of faster and slower balls, but knows when to use them, and who to use them with.

He looks at individual batsmen around the world, plans his tactics, and executes those tactics very well.

Brendon McCullum is a lot younger than me, and my first impression of him, when he joined the Black Caps tour to Australia in 2002, was of a supremely confident young man. It was great to see, in one way, but it was also a new thing to quite a lot of guys in the team. The way he carried himself was probably more the Australian than the Kiwi way.

There are a few of us, including myself, who wish we had a bit more of his confidence. Right from the first game, he carried that confidence with him, and believed in everything he did. Some might call it arrogance, but I think that's much too harsh. To me, it's just self-confidence; he believes in what he's doing, which is why I believe we'll see him succeed a lot more at international level.

He seeks as much information as he can. He'll go to anyone in the team to get as many tips as he can to improve his cricket. Not being shy to seek advice is why I can see him improving in years to come. I know, for example, that he still keeps in touch with Steve Rixon for specialised ideas about keeping.

When you see Baz, as we all know him, away from the game, not as people see him on television, he's a very down-to-earth, really likeable young guy.

It's a shame, in a way, that people can only form an opinion on what they see on television, where he's revved up, as wicketkeepers tend to be, which could lead to entirely wrong conclusions being drawn about what he's really like.

Baz is pretty much in my pocket for the rest of our lives, because I've never let him forget that he's the reason I finished my one-day bowling career on 99 wickets. The last catch ever dropped off me was Wavell Hinds at Eden Park, when Hinds nicked it, and Baz put it down. Cricinfo doesn't suggest it was a big chance, and I never mention all the other catches that other people have put down over more than a decade, but those are mere details when Baz and I have a laugh about it.

In the field, the wicketkeeper is the focal point for the whole team. Go round the whole world and you'll find the same thing. All wicketkeepers are the same. They chat, they chat, they're just a ball of energy. It was Baz's job to keep the energy up, and when I was in the team we fed off him. If he was ever a wee bit flat, quite often so were we. But when he was buzzing, as he usually was, being a little annoyance behind the stumps to the opposing team, then we were up with him.

By and large, the sort of chatter on the field that gets labelled 'sledging' is not as mean or as nasty as it's sometimes presented. Not a lot of it goes on now. It's just to try to get into the batter's head. Yes, you are trying to upset him enough to break his concentration. If you get him out doing it, then so be it, it's worked. He's gone against what he was trying to do.

There will be times when it can get too heated, and sometimes, after the day's play is over, there may have been something said that's regretted. But it is international sport, you want to win, and you're trying to do your best for your country. Sometimes emotions run high. Different guys get more heated than others.

It's just a part of international sport, and with the technology available now it's highlighted a lot more. In my opinion, as long as it doesn't get into areas that are unacceptable, like a player's family, his wife, or his partner, it's good to have a part of the game that's not as buttoned down as a lot of the game is. I feel it's cracked down on too hard. To me, it can be a fun part of the game — not when you're targeted of course, but in general.

Various players have their own way of letting people know they're there. Cairnsy always had a sarcastic edge when he was saying things; Brendon McCullum and Craig McMillan are more straight out in your face.

Among opposing teams, Warney was probably the funniest guy. Maybe there were times when he went a little too far, but generally he was just funny. I always found Glenn McGrath funny, too, although he didn't mean to be. He was a great one for mumbling and swearing under his breath. So it'd be 'effin' this, effin' that, effin' the other thing'. Then he'd put his head down and carry on back to his mark.

I've never done it, and Flem never really has either. The one time with Flem that stands out is that he targeted [South African captain] Graham Smith one year when they were in New Zealand, and you could see them have a bit of a verbal stoush in the middle of the wicket. Smith was out three balls later. Whatever Flem said, and I didn't hear it, I bet he had thought about it carefully — and it worked.

Dan Vettori and I got on pretty well right from the start. When he was first in the team, we were both single, so on tour we'd often head out and enjoy the touring life.

He's always been an intellectual sort of person, who reads widely on all things, not just cricket. At times he's way too clued-up for a lot of us, me included. Some of the jokes he comes up with can sail right over my head, but he's very good fun to be around. Dan just enjoys life.

I do remember the first time he arrived with the team. I think he was a substitute fielder for us in Hamilton, and he turned up, barely 18 years old, with long straggly hair, wearing glasses, as thin as a rake, and it'd be fair to say a lot of us wondered 'What the hell have we got here?'. Of course, he's gone on to prove us all wrong. Dan works almost endlessly at his game, developing his action, just looking for things to make him better.

Mates of his started the Beige Brigade, which has been a fantastic thing, making supporting the team a lot of fun. As players we enjoy them.

Dan comes across as extremely relaxed, but deep down he has a burning desire to do well, and if he doesn't, then, like a lot of us, it eats away at him. As laconic as he can be in interviews, he's a perfectionist when it comes to his cricket, and I think you can see that in the way his batting has improved in recent years. He's now a genuine batter at international level and has played some outstanding innings for us.

He's been the New Zealand vice-captain for a couple of years now, and has to be the captain-in-waiting after Flem, who I'm sure he's learnt a lot off. When Flem was away, I think Dan did an outstanding job, right from the first couple of games.

Because he started so young he's in the middle group of the Black Caps in age, but in experience and maturity he's very much a senior player. The intelligence of the man, and the way he goes about his cricket, means he'll step into the captain's role very nicely.

Craig McMillan and I have known each other from our school days. He was good mates with my brother Daniel, and one early memory is of the two of them coming to our place after school. I'd just started to play for Canterbury, and I had a small collection of bats that I kept in my wardrobe in my room. Macca will hate me saying this, but he never had any qualms about wandering straight in, straight to the wardrobe, picking up every bat in my wardrobe and trying them out for weight and size. That's Macca. Straight in, bull at a gate, no worries.

Our lives have had a lot of parallels. Same school, same cricket club, married sisters, and there have been a few games where we've had similar fates, including a test match at Old Trafford where we both got centuries; and we both got dropped from the Black Caps at the same time as well.

He's a man who wears his heart on his sleeve. He will always let you know what he's thinking — which some might say has been to his detriment at times.

Macca believes so much in what he does. He's been in and out of the New Zealand team, and he's been heavily criticised at times for his approach, for making rash shots, for his technique. But he sticks to what he knows, and it'd take a lot of persuasion to get him to move away from what he's doing. He's stubborn. If he gets an idea in his head, he'll stick to it through thick and thin.

I'm stubborn as well, and it can be a trait that is both good and bad. I know there have been times when I probably should have changed my way of thinking, or tried something different, and I haven't done so. Possibly Macca can also be too hard-nosed sometimes, but when you look at how he got back from the wilderness to having a pretty steady World Cup in the West Indies, it just shows the steel in his character, and how much he believed in himself.

If you don't know him, he can appear to be gruff, even abrasive, but he is a guy who during his career has copped a lot from the media. Some of it was warranted, but some of the really cutting, personal stuff has been unwarranted. We all know that we'll be criticised at times, and if it's fair, about the cricket we've played, I know that I — and this is true of Macca too — have no problem with that. But in the lead-up to the World Cup there were personal attacks on him, even songs written about his weight. To me, it is completely off the mark and unacceptable for people to get on radio and make snide, personal remarks.

I think that's where some of his gruffness with the media comes from, and sometimes it happens with the public too. If you hear a guy on radio ripping into a player, then it tends to give some members of the public what they think is a licence to have a go as well. I don't think you could ever blame someone who is sniped at in public for having a word back.

Christopher Cairns, in his early days, was always going to be given the 'son of', as in 'son of Lance', tag.

Lance had a great career for New Zealand, and after he famously hit six sixes in a one-day game in Melbourne he was a folk hero. But technically, I think Chris was a better cricketer than his dad, and by the end of his career I think he'd dropped that 'son of' tag. I really hope that people remember Chris for Chris, a very, very good cricketer.

I first played against him in an under-age tournament when we were probably only 14 or 15, and he was a lot taller, and a lot stronger than the rest of us little guys. He bowled very quick for our age group, so, even after all these years, I can still remember what it was like facing him. He was a strapping guy with heaps of pace.

When he was injury-free and playing well, Chris was the complete cricketer. He could destroy an attack with his batting, almost at will, and his bowling, especially during his early years in the New Zealand team, was very sharp. But sadly, he had a horrendous run of injuries that prevented him from bowling as fast as he would have liked throughout his career. Fully fit he was a great athlete.

As a batter, he had a heap of natural talent and this, combined with his size and strength, gave him a great advantage — I've never come across a guy who hits the ball as long and as hard as he does. He could have always been in the New Zealand team just for his batting ability alone, but he was so intensely competitive that he would have found it hard not to be able to bowl as well.

In his younger years Chris did have some rough patches off the field, and my feeling is that, when he looks back, there may be some things he might like to have changed. But when John Graham and Steve Rixon arrived in the New Zealand team, he found the right people to work with. That was when I think he found real direction, and he gave a lot to the team, not just on the track, but with the cricketing knowledge that he'd picked up over a long career.

Chris has very strong ideas about how he wants to play the game, but I think before John Graham and Stumper came on the scene, his ideas didn't get listened to. To be fair to Chris, I think he had a good point; that he'd played a lot of cricket, and he should have at least been listened to. Boundaries were put in place by DJ and Stumper, but they would also always listen, even if they didn't adopt what a player was suggesting.

Cairnsy was also a good tourist. He's a lively guy, who, if some entertainment was needed, would lead it, but was also never afraid to delegate — Hamish Marshall was his protégé in that field.

Chris Harris has always been a person with an endless supply of energy. Life is never quiet around Chris. He's cracking a joke, telling a cricketing story, or just acting the fool. He says he's always had energy to burn, and only needs four or five hours' sleep a night, and I can believe that.

In all-round fielding ability, he was just fantastic — the best I ever played with. At his peak, I'd rate Harry as the best fielder in world cricket. People talk a lot about Jonty Rhodes, and what a good fielder he was, and that's true. But if you watched the two, Harry was more of an athlete as far as catching and picking a ball up cleanly. Jonty was a great stopper of a cricket ball, but if you put videos of the two side by side, I believe you'd find that Harry was not only a great stopper, but nine out of ten times would pick it up cleanly, which made him more dangerous to the batting side.

In all the cricket I've played, I'd rate him as one of the most talented players, full stop. But I also think that he never fully realised all of his batting talent. At the World Cup in India in 1996, against Australia in the quarterfinal in Madras, he scored one of the best centuries that I've ever seen, 130 runs, including four sixes and 13 fours, off 124 balls, against an Aussie attack that included Shane Warne and Glenn McGrath. I thought then, 'That's the making of Chris Harris as a batsman'. But he always ended up back down at No. 7 or No. 8, and he became known as the finisher. I always felt that he was better than that.

But for some reason he never got back up into the top of the order. We went through a phase where if we were in the crap at all, Chris would come in and win the game for us. He hit a golden patch, and I guess he got so good at finishing off the game for us that it worked against him being promoted up the order. That was a shame, because I think he had a lot more talent than just being the man that comes in at the end to clean up.

When he batted for Canterbury at No. 4 or No. 5, he usually held that middle order together. Internationally, we saw the best of Chris late in the order, but if he'd been given the chance I think he could have become a hell of a top-order player.

ken Rutherford was the New Zealand captain when I first came into the side, and I always enjoyed his company. When I first got into the team I found him very accommodating; he was welcoming. He enjoyed a beer and going out, but he didn't leave you out in the cold. You felt you were being kept involved, so I was happy with the way he did his job and how he treated me.

There are captains who keep to themselves, especially with the younger players. They have their own circle of more experienced players, and they're the ones they stick with. On the other hand, Ken treated me with complete respect from the time we first met. There are some who say that he wasn't popular with everyone, and there may have been players whose egos were such that they felt he needed to take their approach, which was a bit more lemon-lipped than the way Ken approached things.

He was basically a good keen Kiwi bloke, who could be described as one of the old-school guys round the traps. He just seemed to enjoy everything cricket and a tour involved. My transition into international cricket was made a lot easier for me by the attitude Ken had towards me.

Dion Nash is a man I have a lot of time for. He's probably the most competitive guy I've ever met. Every time he played, he gave it every single thing he had. His intensity in competition was fantastic. Even in warm-ups, he gave it death. We used to play touch football before training, and Dion and Adam Parore were always at each other's throats then. I remember in India how they once almost came to blows during a game of touch.

Dion was one of those guys where you always knew where you stood with him. He wasn't afraid to push you personally, to push the right buttons to maybe piss you off a bit to charge you up. He told you what he was thinking, and he also expected that honesty, even if it was a touch brutal, back from you.

As far as the pushing of team-mates to help get us a competitive edge, he was one of the best I played with. Because he never dropped off in intensity, he had the right to urge others to do the same. He was just a great man to have in our team. It was sad for all of us that he suffered a lot of back injuries that basically ended his career. He was a very talented cricket player, and we missed a lot of great cricket when he was cut down by injury. Dion could bowl, as we all know, but he could bat very well too.

Roger Twose would have been a character in any team. He was one of those guys who just worked out his game to the utmost degree. He knew his capabilities, and he'd work on those strokes day in, day out until he had a game plan down pat. In the last two or three years of his career, he put up some very good stats, which was a measure of how much he'd thought his game through.

Roger was a very good team man. If things were down, he'd always crack a joke, or say something to lift the spirits. He was a very emotional sort of guy, who was not afraid to show it when he was playing. If we were fielding, and things were slowing down, he'd be one who would work to get us back up again. Despite what they say about stiff upper lips, it's my experience that a lot of English people [Roger was born in Torquay in Devon] are like that. They're fun to be around, and get a lot of enjoyment from what they're doing. He became one of our best batters.

I'm a typical New Zealand male, who doesn't show a lot of his emotions in public, yet I actually think it would be a good thing if more of us did show what we felt during a game. People would get a better idea of the different personalities, and I think it'd be a lot more enjoyable for people watching. Of course, if it's not your natural temperament, it's very hard to do. I just think, in general, that Kiwis are pretty conservative, so we grow up holding in what we feel.

The prime example of a cricketer who doesn't hide his feelings is Shane Warne, and he's an exciting player as a result. He is what he is, and he doesn't care — in a good way — what people think about him. Sure, he's done some silly things, and sure, there are some things I'm sure he regrets doing, but he just loves his cricket, and loves life in general. Even with those things he's done that actually aren't right, the fact remains that he's a character, and whether you love him or loathe him, you can guarantee that if he's on television playing cricket, there'll be a good audience sitting down to watch.

Right now, if I sat down and tried to think of other characters in cricket, like, and this is going back a bit, Merv Hughes, I'd struggle to throw one at you. Whether it's the cameras that pick up everything on the field, or the intensity of the modern game, that makes people more aware of their behaviour when they're playing, I don't know, but the characters do seem to be disappearing.

Adam Parore was a very complex sort of character. As far as his glovework went, he was the best I ever played with. I also believe he was a lot better batsman than the figures would show, and as far as his pure cricketing ability goes, he'd be one of the first names you'd put down every time.

I got on okay with Adam, but he wasn't really my cup of tea. He was self-absorbed to a degree that, for me, went a little too far. There is a need for cricketers to be self-centred in order to improve their own game, but for Adam it just seemed to all be about him. At times, I'm not sure that he thought about what he was saying before it was said — so there were occasions when his remarks to other guys in the team were very cutting and that didn't endear him to everyone.

Geoff Allott and I have known each other since we were teenagers. Like Roger Twose, he's a guy that played his cricket with an obvious passion, determined to get the best out of himself. Geoff just kept working and working at his game. He suffered stress fractures to his back, but he wanted to play so much that I can remember him getting needles in his back before he'd go out. He has a lot of energy, is always on the go, and is a lot of fun to be around. It can be hard to get a word in sideways when he's around, and in my memory he's always been right about what he was saying.

The only thing none of us, none of the batsmen anyway, liked about him was having to face him in the nets. At one time or another, there wasn't one batsman who didn't cop a beamer. It was always unintentional, or so he claimed. Some of us had our dark theories about it. What's certain is that every net training session a couple of batters would get one bouncing up straight at the head.

If there was one guy you wanted to see succeed, Geoff would be at the top of the list. He just put everything he had into it. And if you want to know how good Geoff was at his best, check out the statistics for the 1999 World Cup in England. You'll find that he and Shane Warne were the leading wicket-takers, with 20 wickets each. Geoff's came off one less game, at an average of 16.25, with an economy rate of 3.70. Shane's came at an average of 18.05, with an economy rate of 3.82. When you have better bowling figures than Warne at a World Cup, you've been bowling very, very well.

Bryan Young was a guy I thoroughly enjoyed batting with when I was opening in one-day games. Out in the middle, he talked good cricket sense. I learned a lot from him when I started opening. He was a genuine opening batsman, and it was only with hindsight that I realised how much I learned from how he went about his game.

He was never rushed, always composed, and everything about him was immaculate, from his gear to the way he started the innings. The way he went about his game was almost an illustration of how to get it right.

Mark Richardson was an intense, multi-faceted character, who worked on his game almost compulsively. Any chance he got, he would be in the nets. He was a guy that would stay there so long that other players queuing up would have to boot him out to get their chance.

'Rigor' knew every shot that worked for him, and he knew exactly in what areas he should leave the ball alone. He's a likeable guy, and the only downside was that he was so desperate to get it right that he often wanted to talk about the game, trying to find anything that might improve his, and our, performance.

His greatest attribute had to be his mental toughness. He could go out there and bat for hours on end, and if they restricted him to three runs an hour, he'd just keep on doing the same old, same old. Since he's retired I don't think he's been replaced at all, and it'll be a while before we get someone of his quality opening for New Zealand again.

Knowing Rigor as a person, I think that if he'd been given a lengthy chance to play one-day internationals it would have mentally stuffed up his game. He had his test game down pat, to the last inch, but if he'd had to go out and play in a different way in the one-day games, I don't believe he could have married the two styles. I'm sure he'd disagree with me, and would have loved to have played more one-day cricket for New Zealand, but, with the utmost respect, I feel that one-day cricket would have been detrimental to his test career, which was so successful that he ended with a career test average of 44.77. Not bad for an opener.

He was always very nervous before he batted, in and out of the toilet half a dozen times waiting for the start of the match. He used to talk about having a little man on his right shoulder, pouring doubt into his ear, but he obviously fought that little man very well.

A lot of people may remember the sight of Rigor in his beige, stretch-lycra running suit, facing what was supposed to be the slowest man in the opposing side at the end of a tour. To be fair to him, he wasn't as slow as he was made out to be. I don't think he lost many of those races, even with the handicap of a banana taped to the inside of his thigh so that he packaged up better.

To me it was a great thing he brought to the game, and it was a tribute to Rigor that not a lot of guys in the New Zealand team wanted to take him on to get the chance to wear the lycra. One player I clearly remember as not being prepared to go anywhere near a run-through with Rigor was Mr Stephen Fleming. I also know that 99 per cent of the team would have had their money on Rigor.

Scott Styris is a street-smart cricketer who will fight to the end of the day. At the last World Cup he proved how outstanding he can be with the bat, and when you add his bowling skills, it is clear that he's a key member of the New Zealand team. He's a genuine matchwinner when he's on song.

He's also good company, and on the golf course often shows that his sporting skills aren't limited to cricket. I know that a lot of people think it's terrible when they hear him being called 'Pig', and I guess it is a bit tough. But it's not a reflection on him as a person, just a wordplay on his surname, as in Sty, Pig Sty.

Jake Oram is someone who I don't think we've seen the best of yet, which is an exciting prospect for New Zealand cricket. Jake has often been labelled the next Chris Cairns, which doesn't seem to annoy Jake too much, but he is a different cricketer to Cairnsy. Jake's a man who thinks a lot about the game, and if he can keep his injuries at bay he'll become one of the leading all-rounders in world cricket.

At the moment, I think he still doesn't rate himself as much as he could. At times, when he's gone out to bat you can detect a little bit of hesitancy, whereas with the physical gifts he has, I believe he can assert himself and dominate attacks. More recently he has been trying to do just that, and when he gets a real handle on that we'll see some great performances from him very consistently. We've seen glimpses of it, but there's a lot more to come. He's made strides in the last year or so to become harder mentally, and when he has that almost ruth!ess streak nailed down, he'll go to a whole other level.

Jake's also one of the funniest men that I've ever met. He's the joker of the team, whether it's telling the media he's going to cut his broken finger off to get to the World Cup, or using humour to lighten a stressful moment. He's a down-to-earth, funny guy, who only needs to impose himself on the game a little bit more to be the best all-rounder in the world.

Lou Vincent is one of the most talented players I've been in a team with, in terms of the range of shots he can play. I've seen him just destroy attacks; but the thing with Lou is that, to me, he's still learning what his game is. One thing about him is that he does everything at 120 km/h.

He doesn't slow down at all — whether he's playing cricket, or playing golf, or taking on anything, he's going flat out. That can come into his cricket. If he does get into a situation where he possibly needs to rein himself in a bit, he tends to go harder. That can sometimes be a good thing, but to make that next step, I think he has to be aware of when he needs to attack more and when he needs to be more defensive.

I feel for Lou in that he has been in and out of the team, and up and down the order. He's never been given a settled position for a long period of time. He's been told things by selectors which haven't always been followed through on, which has miffed him at times. From what I know of him, he's prepared to bat anywhere in the order they want him to.

I wonder if Lou hasn't been a victim of the policy of keeping players off balance that seemed to come with Ric Charlesworth. There was a one-day game in Wellington against the West Indies in 2006, where Lou had been playing very well in the lead-up to the game. We went down to the stadium, and the team was announced there.

Lou wasn't playing, and Jamie How came in instead. I was staggered. Lou's the sort of guy that thrives on confidence, and if you keep knocking him back, it does start to affect him a little bit, as it does with all of us. It was probably especially tough on him, because he'd been in and out of the team, seemed to have cemented his place, and then was left out again.

Peter Fulton has really impressed me in the relatively short time we've played together. He has a great temperament for a young guy. Nothing seems to faze him, he just goes about his business, keeping everything simple and straightforward. He knows his game well, and he's one guy who, the longer he plays, the better he's going to get. Peter's still learning international cricket, and already his record is stacking up very nicely.

The biggest asset is his temperament. There's no fuss, he just gets on with his job. He has a very dry, but keen, sense of humour, when he's not playing. If he gets nervous, he doesn't show it while he's playing, which is something you need, to be a good international cricketer.

Golden Days

We play so much cricket now that to run through every tour, every test series, every one-day international series would be as exhausting for you as it would be for me. But there are some special games, moments, and series that, for various reasons, I will always remember.

1996: West Indies Centuries

My first full tour, to the West Indies, had some painful personal memories, especially in the first match, against the Vice-Chancellor's XI at Sabina Park in Kingston.

In my younger years I never wore helmets, and if I ever did, it was one without a grille. In general, I never felt comfortable in them, and I had a philosophy that the less gear I had on, the more comfortable I felt.

But before we went to the West Indies I got a helmet with a grille on it, purely because we were going to the West Indies, a place famous for having a lot of very good fast bowlers.

In that warm-up game, I remember walking out to bat, with my nice new helmet on, and facing up to Patterson Thompson who was a big, burly, thickset man. We'd heard about him when we got over there. He would prove to be one of the quickest fast bowlers I would ever face. The wicket we were on that day at Sabina Park looked like a sheet of glass, and it was known for being reasonably quick. There was no grass on it, and it was rock hard. Thompson bowled me a short ball, and instead of turning my head, or ducking down, I sort of looked over my right shoulder, and as I did that I lifted my head up, and exposed my chin.

The ball clattered into the grille, then went through and cut me under the chin. I stood there and my head was ringing a bit. The guy at the other end was Craig Spearman, and he walked up and said, 'Are you okay?'.

I said, 'Yeah mate, we'll just carry on'.

He said, 'Maybe not, because you're bleeding a bit'.

I said, 'No, I'm alright'.

'No you're not, look at your shirt.'

I did, and it was completely covered in blood. Craig had a closer look and told me there was a decent-sized cut under my chin. So I went off, and was taken to the hospital. I've never been great at looking at blood and gore, and I made a point initially of not checking the wound out. But after a while, waiting at the hospital, I thought, 'Bugger it. I'm going to have a look.' I got up to a mirror. It was a good cut alright, and there was some stuff, I don't know what it was, hanging out that obviously wasn't meant to be there. I went as white as a ghost, and had to lie down and have some water. They injected me, stitched me back up, and I went back down to the ground.

Lee Germon had come in to bat after I'd been hit, and he later said to me, 'It was a pretty freaky feeling. When I got out there I looked down at the ground, and there were bits of blood splattered all round the crease where you'd been standing.' That's the only time I've ever had to go to hospital after being hit, or needed stitches.

From that point on in the tour Thompson and I were like a red rag to a bull to each other. He was trying to knock my head off, and I was trying to hit boundaries off him.

I remember the hundreds I made on that tour very fondly because they were back-to-back centuries, and it was against a bowling line-up that had Thompson, Courtney Walsh, Curtly Ambrose and Ian Bishop.

As a young guy playing league cricket in England I went and watched them in test matches, so to play them, even if they were a little bit older, and get two hundreds, was something special to me. Your first test hundred is always going to be something special anyway. Making it in the Windies just made it more memorable for me.

Cricinfo, Bridgetown, Barbados.
Third Day, First Test, April 21, 1996:
A magnificent double-century by hometown hero Sherwin Campbell helped the West Indies build up a massive first innings lead in the First Test against New Zealand.

West Indies was all out for 472 at tea on the third day in reply to New Zealand's first innings total of 195. By stumps the visitors were trailing by 126 runs — although Nathan Astle was still at the crease unbeaten on 82.

It was left to Astle to come to the rescue after New Zealand had slumped to 4/57. Having been badly gashed on the chin by fast bowler Patterson Thompson in the opening tour match a month ago, Astle clearly came out intent on showing that attack was the best form of defence.

He hammered anything loose with ruthless efficiency and all but

10 of his runs came from boundaries — including two massive sixes off Jimmy Adams' slow left-arm bowling.

At the other end, Justin Vaughan remained entrenched for the last two hours and saw off the West Indian attack to make sure he will be still there when the players come out again tomorrow after a rest day.

Cricinfo, Fourth Day, April 23, 1996:

New Zealand began the fourth day 126 runs behind with six second innings wickets intact, and avoided further setbacks in the first hour as Nathan Astle and Justin Vaughan took their fifth-wicket partnership to 144.

Astle was one of three wickets to fall in the morning session, but he had taken his score on to 125, his maiden Test hundred in only his third appearance for New Zealand.

He was out in typically aggressive fashion, aiming a full-blooded drive at Patterson Thompson and was caught head-high at second slip by Sherwin Campbell. His innings had taken only 154 balls and included 22 fours and two sixes.

New Zealand was eventually all out for 305, leaving West Indies a victory target of 29.

Campbell rounded off an outstanding individual performance by making all 29 runs which the West Indies needed to complete a 10-wicket victory over New Zealand in the first Test.

It was possible to score runs quickly in the West Indies. It was the way I played then anyway, but scoring was helped by the fact that the grounds weren't that big, and, with the bowlers setting attacking fields, if you could get past the infield you'd score some runs.

After having been hit by Thompson in the warm-up game, my reaction was to hit back, but I probably went a little too far on the side of scoring freely at every opportunity. They were the sort of bowlers though, that if you didn't attack them, they'd keep on hammering you, until eventually they got on top of you and got you out. If you tried to be a bit more positive, then maybe it'd cause them some doubt and they'd try to change the way they were bowling.

Cricinfo, Second Test, St John's, Antigua.
Third Day, April 29, 1996:
Nathan Astle, the batsman who has been the discovery of the New Zealand season, mounted a lone campaign to save his country on the third day of the second Test against the West Indies.

Astle, 24, was regarded as a one-day slogger when the New Zealanders' tour began but he has now become their most aggressive and successful Test player.

He scored 54 and 125 as New Zealand lost the first Test at Barbados last week, but despite his outstanding example, the remainder of the New Zealand batting is still extremely fragile.

His fighting first innings century helped NZ to 7/346, three runs short of the follow-on mark at the close. Astle produced his second successive hundred to join a select band of 10 New Zealanders to have achieved the feat.

He hit 103 from just 165 balls as the tourists replied to the first innings of seven (declared) for 548 at the Recreation Ground.

The Kiwis resumed on 2/21 and when Astle departed shortly after the second new ball was taken midway through the last session, their chance of avoiding the follow-on appeared in danger.

He was out after a stay of 217 minutes, swinging wildly at Ambrose and getting a thick outside edge for Simmons to make no mistake at second slip. Ambrose was the pick of the West Indies attack with 4/58.

Captain Lee Germon and spinner Dipak Patel then combined in an unbeaten stand of 65 for the eighth wicket to ensure the mark should be a mere formality. Germon, unbeaten on 25, and Patel on 37, survived a hostile final 68 minutes, where they were peppered by short-pitched deliveries from fast bowlers Courtney Walsh and Curtly Ambrose.

Cricinfo, Fourth Day, May 1, 1996:

The second West Indies-New Zealand Test dropped to a slow walk during the fourth day at the Antigua Recreation Ground.

New Zealand finished their first innings not long after lunch at 437, leaving them still 111 runs behind the West Indies first innings of 548 for seven declared.

The pace of the game dropped even further and by stumps the West Indies second innings was at 147 for seven wickets.

A draw will give West Indies the two-match rubber 1–0, but will also represent a fine recovery from New Zealand, who lost the first Test by 10 wickets.

Cricinfo, Fifth Day, May 2, 1996:

Any hope of an exciting, decisive finish to the second and final Test at the Recreation Ground had disappeared by mid-afternoon as the match slowly drifted to a draw.

New Zealand needed 296 runs from 73 overs to produce a win. That task became implausible when they lost three wickets quickly and by tea they were 79 for three.

The match ended in a draw after 65 overs of the New Zealand innings with the Black Caps 130 for five.

1997: Last Ditch Stand

The most unusual batting partnership I was ever involved in was in a test against England at Eden Park in 1997, where Danny Morrison and I managed to get a draw out of what was shaping to be an easy English victory.

By Mark Nicholas, Cricinfo, Auckland, January 28, 1997:

At the evening press conference, New Zealand captain, Lee Germon, said that at around two o'clock, when Danny Morrison, the No. 11, was taking guard, he was wondering how to explain the crushing defeat to the world.

Whatever script he came up with went in the bin because Morrison was still there three hours later when the game was saved. He was pleased with himself was Danny Boy, though he pointed out that he had once batted for four hours and 25 runs in Pakistan, so yesterday's job was a picnic. This, from a man with a world record in Test ducks, 24 in 47 matches — which is a misleading statistic, highlighted by the calamitous fact that Gary Sobers made as many ducks (12) as Bob Willis — and with a testimonial year promotion based around this 'duck' achievement.

In fairness to England, Morrison batted bravely, with considerable nous and with an organised technique which belied his position in the order. He kept his head behind the line of the ball, ignored any temptation outside his off stump and let anything short hit him on the strong shoulders which have carried New Zealand's bowling since the great Hadlee retired.

But Morrison was only a part of the escape story. Nathan Astle, the gifted 25-year-old from Canterbury, was the main thing.

Astle came to the wicket when Germon was left stranded by Adam Parore and run out, then watched as Parore gave his wicket to rampant England.

Astle batted shyly at first, as if a rearguard was beyond him. Then, as he remembered how he had dominated England in Ahmedabad in the first game of the World Cup last February with a brilliant hundred, he began to take control again by pushing the England fielders deep to allow him free singles and puncturing the infield when they closed in to keep him from the strike.

He had the sense to allow Morrison his head by not taking

unnecessary risks to protect him. This gave Morrison confidence and confused England, who did not attack Astle in the way they would have done if he had been with a recognised batsman, concentrating instead on Morrison.

The stroke which brought Astle his hundred, a thunderous drive over extra-cover off Craig White, put the seal on his faultless innings and most important of all had the players on the dressing-room balcony on their feet in acclaim.

In three hours of unlikely cricket, which will have wounded England more than they care to admit, Astle and Morrison recovered New Zealand's spirit.

Danny's record going into the game wasn't flash, with a world record for test ducks, but he was actually a lot better than that. He could use a bat and we actually had a lot of fun out there. Talking with Danny, his attitude was very much, 'Let's just enjoy it'. The longer we went, the more we started to joke about saving the game. That helped take the tension out of it for us. In cricket, as in many sports, you probably play better when you're not so nervous. But it wasn't all plain sailing. The pitch was turning square, and England had spinner Phil Tufnell bowling into a rough patch of the wicket. But while there may possibly have been the odd chance, I can't actually remember one, either from myself or Danny.

I talked to friends in England the next day, who had gone to bed thinking it was all over, then woke up to headlines 'Astle And Morrison Save The Day', which was obviously considered a pretty big feat.

It surprises me that the statistics show that Danny and I shared the number of deliveries we faced evenly. I thought I'd protected him from the strike, but I obviously hadn't farmed it out to the degree I believed I had.

Towards the end, runs started to get important as well as time, so keeping the run rate ticking over was something we were keen to do. When I got to 90, feeling pretty confident that the game had been saved, Mike Atherton, the England captain, came up to me and said, 'Okay, do you want to call it off now?'. I told him in no uncertain terms, 'No thanks, mate, I'm quite happy to stay in and try to get a hundred'. But when I got my hundred that was the end of the match.

Danny Morrison: When I went out I was hoping to stick around long enough for Nathan to get his 50. I never dreamed I'd be there when he got his century.

It was a big effort to draw the test from where we were. I guess that's one of the beauties of the game of cricket, you just never know what's going to happen.

Catches

Taking a good catch is probably the best feeling in cricket. To fling yourself out at the ball, just having a go, and to actually bring it off is very satisfying. I've often fielded in the slips, so there have been a few catches I've been pleased with, but there are two catches in my career that stand out for me and both were made in the outfield. The first was at McLean Park in Napier in 1999, in a one-day international against a touring South African team.

Stephen Fleming: Nathan's deceptively athletic. He's taken the greatest catch I've ever seen, down on the boundary against South Africa, a one-handed catch down on the sight screen running across.

It does come out of the blue. It comes down to that uncanny ability with the hand-eye to pull things off. But it's not just in cricket. He's a very good table tennis player and a very good soccer player. In cricket, you could just see that, when he wanted to, he had the ability to move and look like an athlete. Although, he sometimes chose to stay in third gear until the speed was really needed. But by the end of his career, you almost came to expect him to get the outstanding run out, to pull off a great catch, to do something special with ease.

Cricinfo, Napier, March 26, 1999:

South African cricketer Lance Klusener wields the heaviest bat in the business, and he needed it to slug the Proteas to a dramatic series-squaring one-day victory against New Zealand at McLean Park.

Klusener slammed an unbeaten 35 in 20 balls with four fours and the match-winning six on the game's final ball yesterday from a Dion Nash full toss.

The hearty blow enabled the Proteas to snatch victory from the Black Caps in a see-saw struggle.

The result leaves the teams tied two-all in the six-match BNZ series with the fifth game, a day-night match, in Auckland.

Using the bat more like a club, as Lance Cairns used to wield his Excalibur, Klusener launched into the off-target Nash delivery — he was trying to bowl a yorker — with four wanted from the final ball, and it sailed into the stands.

Nathan Astle had brought the Black Caps back into contention with his miraculous one-handed diving catch which dismissed Sean Pollock at long-on for 16 in the 38th over, which took South Africa to 162/7.

Sean Pollock clobbered one pretty much dead straight down the ground. Dion Nash was bowling and I was at long-on. I just ran as fast as I could and dived at full length. I don't think I could have got any more out of my dive, I stuck out my left hand and the ball just smacked into it. In my memory I slid for three or four metres after I'd taken the catch. The outfield was still a little slippery from rain that had washed out the game the day before.

Chris Harris was running the other way, and when we both

realised it had actually stuck, Harry, taking the mickey, slid along the ground the opposite way, then came to a halt, held out his hand behind his head, his elbow on the ground, and struck a pose. So he was lying there posing, hoping I'd do the same, but I just got up and ran off. I was delighted at having caught the ball and that was all I was thinking of. Poor old Harry posed for a few seconds, then realised I'd got up and run in, so had to leap up before he looked like a bit of a dick.

Everyone was reasonably happy at that point, but Klusener's six just pipped us. They were five runs behind when he faced that last ball.

The other catch that resonates for me was in 2006 at Jade Stadium. The great feeling about that was that it came at a stage where the game was evenly balanced, and helped us get a win.

Cricinfo, Christchurch, February 25, 2006:

Nathan Astle showed he was worth his weight in gold to this New Zealand team, crafting a superb century to take them to a total of 276 and then pulling off one of the most stunning catches you will see in a long time as the West Indies lost a thriller by 21 runs.

When Stephen Fleming won the toss and chose to bat, his biggest worry was how the top order would fare, and those concerns proved to be well founded.

When Peter Fulton chopped Dwayne Smith to Chris Gayle at slip leaving New Zealand at 87 for 4, the West Indies had a strong chance of restricting New Zealand to a manageable score in good batting conditions.

But Astle, a veteran of more than 200 ODIs, knew the score and kept the West Indian bowlers at bay. He realised that the West Indies second-line bowlers posed little threat and simply refused to make a mistake. Initially, he cut out his favourite scoring shots, the forcing drives square of the wicket played with an angled bat, and focused on picking up ones and twos with irritating regularity.

When they quickly accounted for the dangerous Brendon McCullum, run out for only 10, the West Indies were in with a real chance to keep New Zealand down to under 250.

But Astle picked the right time to accelerate, looking for the odd boundary to go with scampered runs, and then ended the innings in a crescendo that got the crowd to their feet. He smashed the last three balls of the innings — bowled by Gayle — for big sixes, and had done his part, taking New Zealand to 276. Astle's unbeaten 118 came off just 126 balls, and put the West Indies on the back foot.

In their innings the West Indies stuttered to 141 for 5 and it would take an extra-special effort for West Indies to reach their target.

The only such effort, though, came from Astle. Smith tried to clatter Jeetan Patel over midwicket, and had timed his hit sweetly. Astle, on the ropes, jumped up, timing his leap perfectly, plucked the ball out of the air, and landed safely within the ropes. Stunned West Indian supporters could only gawk in awe as another wicket fell, with the score reading 153 for 7, and it seemed Astle could do no wrong.

The West Indies would fall short by 21 runs, giving New Zealand the series 3–0.

Dwayne Smith can turn it on and hit boundaries on a quite regular basis. I remember standing out there on the mid-wicket boundary, looking at the way he was batting, and thinking that pretty soon he was going to hit the ball out to where I was standing. No sooner had the thought crossed my mind, just one or two balls later, than that's exactly what happened.

It was either going to be a six, or I might be able to stop it. I was standing as close to the rope as I could, and as the ball came in over my head, I jumped straight up, stuck my right hand up, and caught it. The hardest part was coming back down, landing on my right leg, and trying to balance myself to stay in the field of play.

On replays, if you look at the catch, the arc of my body as I bend back actually takes the ball — in the air of course — back out over the boundary. To come back down straight, and to manage to hold my balance, was something that I was certainly happy about.

We had a fielding coach, an American guy with a baseball background, called Mike Young, who is based in Australia. He used to walk around the ground, and he had this little phrase, 'take a knee', where he'd put one knee on the ground and watch the game like that. He happened to have taken up that pose right next to where I was fielding. So he was pretty happy, yelling and giving me a big American high five.

Once I'd come down, I just ran in with the ball in my hand, not really believing it had stuck. I don't know if the word 'fluke' is fairly applied to catches like that. After all, you do intend to catch them, and while nine times out of ten the ball is dropped, everything you're aiming for is to catch that ball. I've certainly practised fielding close to the boundary, so I'd like to think there's an element of skill in it. The lucky part of a one-handed catch is whether or not the ball actually sticks in your hand. At that stretch you obviously can't use the other hand, so the ball has to strike right in the middle of your palm, and if it's anywhere other than flush in the palm, it'll drop out. But if your timing is right, and that's where it hits, it will stick.

Denis Aberhart: As a fielder he had very, very good hands, and he was much better in the outfield than people gave him credit for. He covered the ground reasonably well, and his pick-up and throw was very quick. So what we saw when he made that catch at Jade Stadium against the West Indies was the determination of the man. A lot of people might not expect that of Nathan, but what he did to take that catch was pure determination.

1999: Series Win in England

Of all the series I've enjoyed, the 1999 series in England means the most to me, for a number of reasons. Before we went away, a tremendous amount of planning went into it, and Gilbert Enoka was very involved, reminding us of the history of New Zealand teams touring England.

We were well aware that only one New Zealand team, in 1986, had ever won a series in England, and not one New Zealand team had ever won at Lord's, where we would be playing our second test in a four-test series. We were touring on the 50th anniversary of the great 1949 team, who had set a benchmark for New Zealand cricket, when the four tests in their series were all drawn. We called ourselves the '99ers.

One of the things we discussed as motivation was who were the people who have inspired us during our life, and in our cricket. My dad was my key figure: with my cricket, he'd been there from day one, always supportive, always helpful. It was also the last tour for Steve Rixon, which made it a very big thing for the team as a whole.

The first test was at Edgbaston, in Birmingham, and we were all gutted when we lost it. And although England won, I imagine that Alex Tudor, who had been the England night watchman and who was left stranded on 99 not out in England's second innings, would have felt a bit the same. England had seven wickets in hand, and Tudor was batting with Graham Thorpe. Instead of hanging back, and letting Tudor get his century, Thorpe just went ahead. I remember being amazed at Thorpe's selfishness.

By Michael Henderson, Cricinfo, July 5, 1999:

If events on the first two days of the Birmingham Test were extraordinary, the resolution on Saturday was baffling.

Showing a breathtaking disregard for everything that had gone before,

Alex Tudor, the Surrey fast bowler, who was sent in as nightwatchman when Alec Stewart was bowled in the first over of their second innings on Friday night, ensured that England won by seven wickets.

Tudor finished one run short of his maiden first-class hundred, and it was a pity that Graham Thorpe, his county colleague, did not push a few balls back to the bowlers, to help him get there.

Tudor, apparently, told him simply to win the match, but it was still a bit of a swizz. He is a young man of 21 and even if he plays Test cricket for another 10 years he may never come as close to making a hundred.

The second test was at Lord's, and it was huge. It was without question one of the most special moments I enjoyed in my career. For the New Zealand team to go to the home of cricket and finally win a test match — bringing the series back to one-all — was massive. I clearly remember sitting up on the balcony when the winning runs were hit, and how all of us were leaping up and down, just loving the whole thing.

Lord's is a hard thing to explain in many ways. There's so much atmosphere, so much tradition, so much that's almost mystical about the place. In my entire career I only played two tests there, which is not a lot, and that made it even more special for me and several of the other players.

Before the test, Steve Rixon had sat us all down and gone round individually asking what we could do to go to the next level. Cairnsy jumped up and said, 'I'll be on that honours board at the end of the game. I can't tell you whether it's going to be the 100 or the five-for but I will be on that board.' Sure enough, we had England going from their first innings, when Cairnsy took six for 77 (and made the honours board), and they were all out for 186. We made 358, including a hundred from Matthew Horne, and when they were out for 229 in the second innings, we only needed 58 for the win.

Kiwis Claim Historic Win

New Zealand wrapped up their first ever Test match victory at the home of cricket, Lord's, as England were dispatched in comprehensive fashion on the fourth day.

Matthew Bell hit the winning runs to give the Kiwis a nine-wicket victory, and only their third Test success on English shores.

New Zealand passed their victory target of 58 in the evening session, after dismissing the home side for a meagre 229 before tea.

It was a thoroughly deserved triumph for Stephen Fleming's team, who had out-played England throughout the four days.

'Great players go through New Zealand history and never achieve a win at Lord's and for us to do it is emotional,' said a delighted Fleming.

BBC July 25, 1999

The third test was at Old Trafford, where we fired England out for 199, and then scored 496 in our first innings. I got my only hundred of the series and Craig McMillan scored a hundred as well.

Sadly, rain had a major effect on the game, which was very stop-start as a result.

By Michael Richardson, Cricinfo, Third Test, Old Trafford, Third Day, August 7, 1999:

'Cricket Just Got Better' proclaims a Channel Four poster near Old Trafford, but England's only response has been to get spectacularly worse. England were at the bottom of their game and New Zealand at the top of theirs even before the tourists batted their way into a position from which an innings victory could all too easily follow.

They are a young and inexperienced team from the smallest of Test-playing nations: Before this match their players had scored only two more Test hundreds than Mike Atherton off his own bat.

It is no compliment that England carried on from where they had left off on Friday, most ordinarily. Andy Caddick's first three overs cost 17 as Nathan Astle seized the advantage more like a modern Australian than a New Zealander of old. So again England's spinners had to come on and bowl without pressure on the batsmen or a close-set field.

The start had to be delayed until 11.45 after heavy rain in the night had made the outfield soggy, and from then until 3.20 the crowd of 10,000 had to wait for some reason to applaud England. By then Matthew Bell and Astle had added 153 for the third wicket, and at the goodly rate too of three runs an over.

Even after his 26 not out to knock off the runs at Lord's, Bell's Test average was no higher than 11 before England went to work in this match to make a batsman of him. By the time they had finished every member of New Zealand's eleven here had a Test score of at least 70.

Astle is a player of rough technique and fine eye as well as the urge to dominate. Peter Such had found the right speed to bowl on this pitch earlier than Phil Tufnell, and Astle made sure the Essex off-spinner did not get on top yesterday by twice pull-driving him for six.

Whereas crease-occupation was once the objective of New Zealand's batsmen, they kept on looking to score after Bell and Astle had both gone, the latter to a fine catch off a mishooked ball, after reaching his fifth Test century (101).

Their Australian coach Steve Rixon has instilled in them the self-belief which led him to say soon after his appointment: 'If I was playing for New South Wales second XI against Australia, I'd still think that I'd win.'

Cricinfo, Day Five, Old Trafford:
In this depressing, though illuminating, Test, New Zealand have bettered England in every respect.

Frankly, England don't deserve a draw. The cricket they have played has been so poor, and the manner in which they have played it so listless, that they deserved to lose. Or, to put it more charitably, the spirited New Zealanders deserved to go one up in the series.

The night before the last day of the last test at the Oval we had a team meeting. We needed to win the game to win the series. We hadn't had a great test to that point, but were lucky enough to have the test in the balance. I remember Dion Nash standing up and in no uncertain terms telling us we had to pull our 'beep beep' fingers out. Someone had to stand up and take the game by the scruff of the neck and win it, and the series, for New Zealand.

The next day, he was the man who essentially did just that. For the speech alone, I'd give Nashy the accolades for getting us over the line. He made the hair on the back of everyone's necks stand up, and we just wanted to get out there and do it. I have never heard such raw feeling, such a burning desire to win the game. It was inspiring. He didn't just get up there and ramble on. It wasn't just pretty words. He meant everything he said and you just knew it was straight from the heart. That was him really, a guy who didn't try to hide his emotions, and one of the best cricketers I ever played with.

When we'd won the game, we had to walk up stairs to the presentation on a balcony at the Oval, and when we looked out at the ground, the amount of Kiwi support that was there was remarkable and it was quite moving. Then, when we got back to the shed, it was very emotional. In those days, after a test match win we would go round the room and each guy would mention something that was special to him from the test match.

Several of us had tears in our eyes, not only for the fact we'd won the series, but also because it was the last time we'd have Stumper coaching or DJ Graham as our manager. The atmosphere was electric.

Partners

The Wanderers ground is basically a bowl with stands at both ends, and when you're playing in it, it feels like the whole crowd is in there, right on top of you. When you get a packed-out South

African mob there — always parochial and never shy of a word from the boundary — it can get intimidating.

I remember vividly that that was how it was for our pool game with South Africa at the 2003 World Cup. They batted first, and, fielding at slip, I caught Graeme Smith off just the third ball of the first over — only to find that the umpire had called a no ball. They notched up plenty. Herschelle Gibbs knocked up 143 [off 137 balls], and they posted 306, which in those days was a huge score.

Craig McMillan opened with Flem, and I was at No. 3. They put on 89 before Macca went. I had a weird start. The first run I scored was a single, but I ended up getting five when the return to the bowler's end hit my bat, and the ball ricocheted to the boundary. At first, Steve Bucknor, the umpire, wasn't going to give me the extra runs.

Now, there's a gentlemen's agreement that if a return throw hits you or your bat and flies away, you don't run. But if it hits your bat and runs to the boundary, that's just tough luck. It's in the rules. Of course, no one sets out to hit the ball from a throw in the field, and all I was thinking about was trying to get a single to get off the mark — no thought at all of trying to hit the ball. Flem was able to point out what was right, and Bucknor gave us the extra runs.

I remember that partnership with Flem with special pleasure. It was very satisfying to be batting with an old friend, together in a hostile environment, and to bat well and win the game in a World Cup. The way Flem compiled his hundred was him at his best. South Africa is a tough place to tour, so to have done well there made it one of the most satisfying afternoons of cricket I've ever had.

Cricinfo, World Cup, Pool B, South Africa v New Zealand, Johannesburg, February 16, 2003:
New Zealand batted in a sublime manner, and none more than their captain Stephen Fleming, who truly played the finest innings

of his career, as they took a nine-wicket win over South Africa in a remarkable match at the Wanderers ground.

What emerged in Johannesburg, under absolutely desperate circumstances, was the full flowering of Fleming's abilities, as he scored 134 not out off 132 balls, the highest score of his One-Day International career.

The target of 307 was a daunting one, despite the smaller boundaries of the Wanderers and the pitch, which certainly tamed the New Zealand bowlers and took much of the sting out of the South Africans.

Fleming played shots of authority all around the ground. Initially, he peppered the wide open space in the third man region with safe shots which took full account of the fast outfield, even in the rain that fell at times.

He hit some powerful shots square of the wicket on the leg side, and some remarkable shots through long-on and wide mid-wicket off the back foot that were the perfect summation of a batsman in full harmony with his game.

Fleming and Nathan Astle soon got working in the same way that Craig McMillan had managed in the opening partnership of 89, at which point McMillan was out for 25 off 32 balls.

When Fleming got to 70 it was his highest World Cup score, 86 was his highest score against South Africa.

And in the 30th over, he brought up his century, the fourth and finest of his career, off 109 balls and including 17 boundaries.

The rains came again soon after and New Zealand were 182 for one wicket, with Fleming 104 and Astle on 37 when they left the field.

The game was reduced to a 39-over contest which left New Zealand needing to score 44 off 51 balls.

They only needed 38 balls to do it, Fleming 134 not out, Astle 54 not out, leaving fans at the Wanderers Stadium stunned and wondering how South Africa could lose after scoring 306 runs.

My Way

If you looked closely at how I bat, you would soon see that I'm not technically correct. I never have been, and I've never professed to be. But I was fortunate to have good hand-eye co-ordination and have always just found that what I did mostly worked. People have argued that if I had a more orthodox technique it would have taken me less time to get out of the odd rut that I fell into. That may be true, or may not be. I think every batsman in the world goes through bad form ruts, and they're just part and parcel of the game.

I always knew that I was in good nick when I was leaving balls outside the off stump. Once that happened, the tension lifted, any criticism I was getting stopped, and cricketing life went on. It isn't that I didn't have the chance to change how I batted. Along the way there have been excellent coaches near at hand, but when I look back it's been mainly me forming the way I wanted to play.

Dad coached me, but he let me take my own way. He let me develop my own style. Even through age group and high school stuff, while coaches certainly gave me input, up to when I got into the Canterbury squad I was still developing my batting the way I wanted to. There was coaching in school holidays, and in age group teams from Nicki Turner and Bob Carter, but overall I tried to stick to my own ideas and style.

I had boyhood idols — Ian Botham and Viv Richards were the big ones — but the way I bat is not a reflection of how they played the game. I would look at other cricketers, people like Martin Crowe, and might pick out something they were doing, try it out, and if it worked, continue with it. But, to be blunt, I don't think the coaching manual these days is correct, full stop. I think I'm not the only player around the world who thinks that. I certainly hope I'm not anyway. But when I look around, it is clear that many batters — including many top-class players, like Ricky Ponting — press forward first, which goes against the manuals.

I never had a coach who wanted me to make wholesale changes. On the other hand, I've fiddled with things right through my career. Although one thing that's never changed is that I don't move my feet before the delivery of the ball. In fact, I try to stay as still as I possibly can.

There were times when I got out of nick and felt like my feet were in concrete boots, and I tried to just get a little press forward, just to try to get something going. I worked on that a lot when Stumper was our coach. I also worked with Martin Crowe, who always stressed the importance of balance and being light on your feet. But other than that, there wasn't a hell of a lot of technical coaching.

My feet and my head were such big keys in my game, that if my head was getting dragged across to the off side too early, even only slightly, my feet would follow my head. That's why, when I was in a patch of bad form, I tended to want to go at the ball, to feel the ball on the bat. Obviously, there was a little bit of anxiety and nerves, and that would lead me to drag my feet across the stumps, and I would get out lbw or nick balls that I should have been leaving.

These were virtually the only things I really tried to focus on during my whole career. My head had to go down the wicket towards the other set of stumps, so that my feet would follow and I wouldn't be dragging my feet across the line of the delivery. As I say, it was something I had to work to control throughout my whole career. Other than that, there were a few times when I started to think about my backlift, to try to give myself more time. That was something I thought about mainly when I was out of nick. But I'd always come back to my key points, my head and my feet going down towards the stumps.

Towards the end of my career, I started to think about getting older and my reflexes starting to slow down. I looked around the world, and watched other batters who I admired. Every one of them had his bat up before the ball was delivered. If you ever watched me on video, and froze the replay just before the ball is about to come out of the bowler's hand, you'd see that my bat is still on the ground. I can't find anyone else in world cricket who does that. The closest was Adam Gilchrist.

But most players had their bats either at waist height or were starting to move as the delivery was being made; some guys even stood with their bats up. So I thought, okay, maybe that's giving them a bit more time, because their bat is starting to move before the ball's even released. I started to fiddle with that near the end of my career. Once again, it was when I was going through a bad trot and nothing changed. So, once again, I ended up back where I started.

Out of my whole career the biggest regret I have is that when I went into a bad spell I would often think about everything else, but not the things I should have been, which for me is the head, the feet and the ball. While coaches would never force me to make any particular change, they would give me things to work on, suggesting I try this, maybe this would help, and that's when I could get sidetracked.

If you're going out to bat thinking that you've got to get your bat up, you've got to do this, that, and the other thing, then suddenly the ball's on you, and you're still working things out. There's a state you get into when you're playing well, where everything seems to slow down; well, when you're the other way, everything seems to be happening at 100 miles an hour, and that's when you get into trouble.

For me the two most successful shots I had were the cover drive and the cut. I don't think that either was really technically correct to the purist. For some reason or another I tended to be able to cut the ball that was very close to me. It got me in trouble a few times, but I also got a lot of runs from it. If you look at my balance, when I'm driving my front leg tends to be quite straight — the textbook says it should be bent — and my balance is more central, rather than forward. I was also unorthodox in that I usually played the cut shot off the front foot, as well. I never went back, and across, and cut the traditional way.

I can't explain where it came from. That cut shot, especially, was one that I can't remember practising. I just had it throughout my whole career, but I'd never really trained to come up with the cut off the front foot.

But a shot I did train to develop, the only one, was charging down the wicket. That was a shot I had reasonable success with, and I regularly trained at that in the nets. I'd run at the bowlers, trying to get the right line to run down the wicket so that I would be in the right spot to hit the ball to the area I wanted it to go. To hit it straight, I'd go straight down the line of the stumps; while I would move outside my leg stump to hit it more over cover.

So there were little things like that, where you train to find out exactly where you've got to be to hit the ball into the right areas.

The one-day game has had a massive impact on the range of strokes now played in the game. And the Twenty20 game is moving the game forward even more. I think it's going to become even more advanced. A player like Adam Gilchrist, who some might say isn't always technically correct, is one of the best strikers of the ball ever, in world cricket. Some guys are now so good, and are playing so much cricket, that I don't say they invent shots from scratch, but they come up with ways in the nets, trying to get into a position to hit bowlers, that might not have been thought of before. Then, when you play so regularly, the unorthodox shots become another part of your game, and that's why I think the game's starting to move on a lot more.

In test match cricket now, the speed teams score at means that a lot of tests don't go the full five days. The scores are similar to those made in the past, but the runs (and I suppose the wickets) are coming at a much quicker pace.

I enjoy my one-day cricket more, purely in terms of the fun in the game, but as a test of physical and mental skills, you can't go past a test match. Looking back on playing for New Zealand, I was lucky enough to play 83 tests, but that was over a 12-year period. In my opinion, we don't play enough tests. And then, when we do have a series, it's often just two matches, which, to me, is nuts. I think you've got to play at least a three-test series.

Most of the tests I've played at home in recent years have been part of a two-test series, followed by a group of one-day games. It would have been nicer to play a three- or five-test series, which is the biggest challenge an international cricketer faces.

As I say, however, I probably had more sheer fun in the one-day games. I just liked the one-day games because they were exciting and usually a lot more entertaining for the crowds — and that was something I really enjoyed. The crowds you get for one-day matches definitely add to the atmosphere, and it's a shame that live crowds for all sports in New Zealand, not just cricket, seem to be dwindling. We tend to follow a team if they're doing well. We'll pack out the stadium then, but if they're not doing so well, we stay away, and wait for them to improve.

In other countries we've been to, whether their teams are doing well or not, their crowds are massive. The bigger populations certainly have something to do with it, but I remember back in the 1990s that the crowds we were getting to the Shell Cup were huge, over 20,000. Now you can go down to a provincial one-day game, and you'd be lucky if there were 500 people there.

I remember Rod Latham having a benefit game at Lancaster Park, and a crowd of about 20,000 turned up for that. Now, you'd be doing well to get that to an international match. It may be a sign of the times; there are a lot more things for people to do and the tickets haven't become any less expensive, but the fact is that the crowds are certainly getting smaller.

When you have a big crowd, it livens up everything. When you field on the boundary you can hear the crowd — sometimes hurling a bit of abuse at you. I don't get involved with that, no matter what they're saying. In Australia, it's going all the time. They're shouting, 'We've got club cricketers better than you, Astle' or 'Your girlfriend's a sheep', and it's entertaining to listen to what these drunken people come up with. You couldn't take offence; they're just people having a few beers, having a good time, and having a crack at you because you're from another country. I found it good fun. I never turned around and got involved with the crowd, but I found it fascinating what would come out of people's mouths while they were sitting in the stands. It was different in India, where they're just cricket nuts. Over there, the crowd would tend to just talk to you normally on the boundary, so you would find yourself actually turning round to have a bit of a chat.

If there's a big crowd, and you're going well, then when you're in New Zealand, and the crowd's behind you, it can't help but pump you up and get you even more into the game.

I went through quite a few stages with fitness. When I first started, I found that I was physically okay simply from the sports I'd played for many years. Then David Trist took us on a pre-season tour to South Africa with Canterbury, and while we were there I think I put on about 5 kg in three weeks, purely from drinking alcohol.

There was a photo, which I've managed to get rid of, where I'm standing at the top of a mountain next to Rod Latham, who was playing at the time. Rod, who commentators loved to call 'the chunky Rod Latham', will hate me for saying this, but there wasn't a great deal of difference between us as far as size goes. I remember seeing that picture and thinking 'Holy hell', so from then on I tried to get into the gym more. Earlier in my career, I was never a huge gym person, but then, as I got older, I had two knee operations, and after that I was more dedicated to the gym and thoroughly enjoyed it.

I got into a lot of boxing with Kevin Barry Snr, out at Belfast, with Shane Bond. Of all the fitness I've done, that had the most impact. We also had some sessions with All Black selector Wayne Smith, who also used it for his fitness. When he wasn't away with the All Blacks he'd join us. That was really enjoyable. I've got a lot of time for Kevin Barry. He was a huge help in getting myself and Shane back to full fitness.

They had a circuit going where you'd be on a rebounder, you'd do press-ups, you'd hit the bag, you'd use a medicine ball, and all at reasonably high intensity. The first time we did it, we got to about nine minutes and Shane and I had to stop. I've got a lot of respect for boxers now, and what they go through to get into the ring.

I've managed to keep up my gym work, largely because I was getting older and with the amount of cricket that was being played, you had to try to stay in good shape.

In the Black Caps we all had our own individual regimes we would follow. On tour, a fitness trainer would go away with us, then when we were back in Christchurch we'd touch base with Warren Frost, our fitness guy. He'd put me on a programme, and would check that I was doing things the right way. But in general, the actual activity — going to the gym and doing the work — is left to each player to do unsupervised. That's only come in over the last five years. When we first started there were fitness sessions, but there was no such thing as a cool-down, or stretching, at the end of the day. It was straight back into the shed for a beer.

I'm more of an old-school cricketer, so I was someone who enjoyed the way it was. I was happy to try those things, the warm-downs, the debriefs, the hot and cold baths, even though I was opposed to them. I guess they reached a stage, when John Bracewell was in charge, where they thought I wasn't open to change. But I don't think there was ever something I didn't try, and if it wasn't me, I had to keep going on, even if there wasn't any personal benefit. There were possibly benefits for other players from it all, and I didn't want to discourage anyone else who may have found it worked for him.

Three or four times a year, our fitness levels would be tested. We'd have fat tests, beep tests for endurance, and speed tests to make sure we hadn't dropped off but had been doing the work we should have been.

On the mental side of the game, I've worked a lot with Gilbert Enoka, so we've got to know each other very well. He's brilliant at what he does. His role covers your planning, preparation, and your visualisation, all the sort of stuff that can give you an edge at international level. Gilbert's great skill is that he monitors you as a person, and only gives you advice that he thinks will benefit you, and in a way that you'll be happy to take on board. He doesn't lay down the law and say this is exactly what you have to do. He makes suggestions on things that may help. I have a lot of respect for how he's able to read individuals that way, and how he approached the role.

These days there is usually a group debrief on each game, with a lot of emphasis on a senior players' group, who try to guide younger guys through and help them benefit from the older players' experience. There's also a lot of peer assessments. The way that works is that a group of guys will assess you while you're out of the room, and they'll tell you their thoughts when you're back.

I had some problems with this: the debriefing and talking about the cricket. Sure, if things aren't going well, you've got to look at what you can do to make it run better. But to me, cricket, and a lot of the things that happen in it, often can't really be dissected and explained. Things happen for no logical reason.

We started having more discussions inside the team when [coach] Steve Rixon and [manager] John Graham came on board. Prior to that, there had been a rocky period that did need to be cleaned up. It was a time when there was no real clear direction in the team. When Christopher Doig became the chief executive, he got Steve, John and Gilbert Enoka involved and they had a huge impact on how New Zealand cricket started to go from then on.

We started debriefing when Gilbert was on board. He had the knack of doing just enough, not going into overkill. I know that Steve Rixon wasn't a big fan of debriefs, but he went along with it, and he started to get a lot out of it as well.

That was when it started, and from then on each year there just tended to be more and more, and more. If you open up a forum for everyone to have their say, we all have different ideas and you can end up sitting there for an hour and a half debating why this or that happened — and it can go on for what feels like forever. The danger is that you can walk away with your mind clouded, wondering, 'What actually happened in that meeting? What are we getting out of it?'

To me, there wasn't a lot of point sitting in a room for all that time, going over every little point in the game. It's moved on now to the point where New Zealand Cricket have an Aussie guy, Kraig Grime — who does a lot of work with various sports in Australia — to facilitate the peer assessments. I don't totally disagree with that; I think it's good to have feedback. You might think one way, but others might see it from a different perspective. But there's a lot more to it now. You sit down in a team meeting and you've got to rate your team-mates on a scale of one to ten, and if you rate him under five you have to explain why.

To me, it's not the Kiwi way to sit there and say it directly to someone's face, even though perhaps you should — we're usually a bit more reticent than that; not that we'd go behind someone's back either. You'll say it and there will be a lot of guys who will take it personally, when it's not intended to be personal. The way this sort of feedback is run is vitally important, and that's where Gilbert Enoka, who is no longer with the team, had a real knack of getting people to say things to people's faces in a way that wasn't taken personally.

To me it's getting to a point where there are just so many meetings about everything other than just playing the game. It's vital you get the right people to run these sessions. I don't think John Bracewell is skilled enough to do this particular job, whereas Gilbert knew just when to stop things, when to keep things going, he just had a good feel for it. We used Gilbert pretty much fulltime for quite some time, and then he was sought after by the All Blacks, and the time he spent with New Zealand cricket dwindled. Other people tried to fill that gap, but in my opinion there's no one that's actually made things work as well as he did. They've tried their hardest to get it right, but, to me, they haven't got the skill to do it.

When Steve Rixon, John Graham and Gilbert were running the team there wasn't, in fact, so much emphasis on peer review. Assessment was more concerned with the running of the team. You'd have Steve Rixon saying, 'Okay guys, what went well, what went wrong today?'. Knock that on the head, move on. In the last two years there has been a tendency to try every new thing that someone gets hold of.

The senior players' group was set up by Gilbert, and when he left, the guys in the group — Stephen, myself, Dan Vettori, Shane Bond and Jake Oram — tried to carry it on. But I don't think we had the skills to do so. We would sit down and talk about cricket, but to me it was just another talk about cricket for the sake of it. Gilbert would guide us, ask leading questions, ask us to look at what we thought might work, would it be better another way? He didn't have us holding back. It was straight at you, but the way it was delivered was such that you'd pause and think, 'Okay, I don't actually agree with you, but I'll think about that'.

An example of how it goes wrong without the right people there came during my last year in the team at one of our peer reviews. There was a formula that gets used in one of these review exercises where you are told three words that sum up what the guys think of you, as well as something you've got to start doing, something you've got to keep doing, and something you've got to stop doing.

In our group we were talking about one of the younger players, and he smokes a bit. The issue was raised by management. They said that one of the things they wanted the player to stop doing was smoking.

I sat there and we carried on talking about it, but it didn't sit well with me. It was an odd one for me, because I don't smoke, and I don't agree with smoking, but, as I see it, we're grown men and it's your choice. I said that I disagreed with what was going on. I said, 'I don't think that we can sit here and tell a guy to stop smoking. For a start it's a lot harder to do than we might realise. And if you start doing that in these peer reviews, tell a guy to stop smoking, where does it stop? Who are we to tell guys to do that?'

There were other things mentioned. Do we police guys' sexual behaviour? We train in singlets with the threat of UV rays. Do we ban that? It's a fine line between trying to change a person from who he is to trying to help him grow as a person. I had a big problem with sitting there, trying to tell this guy to change his personality. I really felt, who were we to do that?

Of course, it could have been mentioned, as something to consider, but I had a problem with setting rules for someone else. He has a cigarette before he goes out to bowl or bat, which is telling me that it calms him down.

Now in my view that's not the ideal preparation, because I don't smoke, but if it helps him to go out and perform, then who am I to tell him to stop doing that?

It's a question of where you draw the line; I believe that this sort of feedback needs to stick to what's going to benefit a person in cricket first of all, and then, if he's got some glaring problem, such as being on the turps until three o'clock in the morning, then sure, you need to address it.

But, in general, I think you have to watch that you don't start to clone guys, that you allow for individuals to still be themselves, you don't force people into behaviour that's laid down by the rest of the group.

If there's something that's upsetting a team, then it has to be stopped. I'm not saying that having a stricter regime is wrong, but for me personally I don't like to see a team get too buttoned down.

I look at a young guy like Ross Taylor, who is dynamic, has everything going for him, and I'll watch with real interest to see where he goes. The senior guys should guide Ross, try to help him in every way they can, but don't let him lose what he's got, which is something special and unique to him.

I've been in and out of the senior players' group — who really want it to work — but we don't have a person there all the time to fine-tune it. Obviously, there are financial issues for New Zealand Cricket, which may be the reason there's not an expert available fulltime, but I don't see much point in plugging away at something that isn't working.

One of the things I disagreed with was that over the last couple of years we had guys popping in and out, even to the point where our management team, the trainer, the physio, the people helping us with a mental side of the game, were there and then they'd be gone. There'd be a new physical trainer for every tour, which made it like a new start every time: the new guy had to get to know the team and he'd have different ideas from the guy before.

So it was one step forward, two steps back. I couldn't help but notice that other teams seemed to have the same backup group travelling with them for a number of years. This is particularly important, I believe, for the bowlers, especially the fast bowlers, who can easily pick up injuries if things aren't done just right. I think it is crucial that our physical trainer actually gets to know Shane Bond, and what works for him, and to understand the regime he's on.

Sure, a new guy will be briefed, but they all have their own ideas, and they always want to put their own stamp on it. In theory, there's nothing wrong with that, but I think in a cricket team that that's not the way it should be. To me, the longer you can keep a guy in the support group, the better he gets to know who will play through a twinge, how guys will react to pressure and injuries, and all of that is an important but often underrated part of keeping a team going.

Glenn Turner: I fully understand his feelings about long debriefs and so on. What's happened is that we have all these 'add-ons' as I call them, who are trying to justify their positions, and I found, even at the provincial level, you had to try to undo some of the work that had been done by others, by letting people express themselves without endless analysis on what should or shouldn't be happening, what's gone on and so on, by allowing people's natural talent to come through.

I believe that after they're about 17 or 18, players have been doing what they've been doing for so long, that you're talking about minor refinements and maybe an attitude change or two, and, frankly, that's about it.

I can understand exactly where Nathan's coming from. But what can happen then is that people around him start saying, 'Aw, Nathan's not a thinker, he's pretty straight-forward and he doesn't look into the complexities', as though he doesn't have the intellect to do it.

That's a criticism I disagree with. He may not want to go into the details of a lot of things, but one of the secrets and skills is to narrow down what really counts, and what really is important, and to try to discard all the rest of the crap. You can reach a stage of information overload, which leads to paralysis by analysis.

The more I learn about this game, the more I realise that the secret is to reduce, to precis everything to the key areas. Most coaches, and people involved in the game, are almost boasting about their knowledge, and are doing more harm than good.

For example, I've discovered that there's no scientific evidence that ice baths do any good at all. I've never met a medical expert who believes it benefits a player. The only good that I can see is that it's a really good discipline, and you might even see it as a punishment.

I know that Jeff Wilson, when he was playing rugby for Otago, refused to do it, and they accepted the fact that he wouldn't do it. As for these warm-downs, in cricket you might have been standing around for three or four hours. If you were being slightly facetious, you could argue that the game of cricket is a warm-down in itself compared to other sports.

Dropped

'Shocked' would be a good word to describe my feelings when I was dropped from the Black Caps in December 2005. I'd been lucky enough before then to have only ever been dropped once or twice in my whole career. Looking back, and considering what we do for a living, I suppose I've been lucky.

Black Caps coach John Bracewell told me in a phone call that my services were not going to be required for the first Sri Lankan series. The main reason, I was told, was that I'd struggled with the bat, and they wanted me to go back to first-class cricket to get some runs under my belt. That was fair enough. They also wanted to try a couple of younger guys in those positions to create some depth in our team.

John was very matter of fact and I was probably short with him, as I just said, 'Thanks very much, see you later'. I was with my wife, Kelly, and we were out shopping at the time. I got off the phone and said to her, 'I'm not in the team'.

I think she was as stunned as I was. One of the main reasons that it came as a shock to me was that I thought there were one or two guys who, in my opinion, were in worse form than me at the time — and probably in worse form than Craig McMillan, who was also dropped.

The first person I texted was Flem. I wrote, 'I've been left out'.

His reply, as I remember, was, 'Have you really?'.

From what I can pick up, when he left me two or three days earlier he'd thought I was in the frame for the 12 or 13 guys they were going to have in the team.

Let me explain some of the background. We'd gone to Zimbabwe towards the end of 2005, and I'd scored a century in one of the two test matches we won. Then we moved on to South Africa, and in four one-day games my best score had been 37.

We came home, and played Australia three times in the Chappell-Hadlee series. Once again I was pretty scratchy. I got a couple of 14s and a 22.

With hindsight, the way I'd been approaching my batting in the few months before I was dropped, hadn't been how I usually played the game. It was a bit more circumspect, and, maybe because I was struggling a bit with my form, I was trying harder, and working harder, as you do, to get back on track. Sometimes, in those circumstances, it's difficult to go back to using your natural talent and just trusting what you've got.

Looking back on it, maybe I was in a bit of a rut and working too hard on my game. That's never been me. Sure, you have to work at some things, but I was spending a lot longer in the nets, trying different things, and that wasn't what I should have been doing. As a cricketer, if you're missing out on big scores you know there's always a chance that you might miss out on the team. That thought might have been in the back of my mind. But there were also other guys in the team — without naming names — who had been struggling longer than I had.

John Bracewell: Dropping Nathan was a twofold thing. One was that I needed to increase the depth of our squad, as I was planning for the World Cup. The other was that I needed to lift Nathan's energy in order for him to be as effective and as fearless as he had once been at international level.

I felt that he was taking fewer risks than he once had. He was becoming a little more conservative. I needed that fearlessness of his, where he would come down the wicket and charge bowlers, smacking them over the top, and wanted to get that accelerated, fearless start back into him. I also felt that he'd lost a little bit of his intent.

But they were two separate issues. The larger picture was that we needed to increase the depth in the side, and at that point I needed to have at least two options in every position. Opening in one-day games was a position we were quite weak in. Stephen and Nathan had dominated that position in one-day matches, but never did it in tests. So we didn't have guys who could transfer over from test matches to one-day games, so overall we were quite weak in numbers in that particular area. That was the reason for advancing Lou Vincent up to opening the batting in one-day cricket.

We weren't sure, either, how long Nathan's knees would last, so we needed that contingency planning in the whole process. That went through a number of other positions as well.

I also needed to try to reignite the spark in Nathan, which I thought at the time was starting to dwindle.

The rest of the day the media were after me. But I told New Zealand Cricket that I wasn't interested in any interviews and didn't talk to them.

Pretty much the whole day was spent in a state of shock. Given the stage I was at in my career, thoughts of retirement did jump very strongly into my head. I was thinking about that a lot. And the more I thought about it, the more it seemed that, at the age I was, and with the selectors wanting to try some younger guys, perhaps there was more to it than simply being dropped to regain form. I just wanted to sit down with Gilbert Enoka, who is a very good friend, to chew the fat with him about where I was and where I was going to go with my career. Later that afternoon when we did sit down together, I did start talking about retirement.

I think it was the next day that I got a message on my phone from Braces, saying, 'Don't do anything stupid'. Whether Gilbert had talked to him or not, I don't know. But it was a good message to get from the national coach, and eased my concerns a little.

Without being exact about the dates, I'd say that for at least a week I was close to pulling the pin on the game of cricket. I must have talked to Gilbert three or four times during the week. I wanted to work through things without undue haste. Obviously, there is an emotional reaction when you first get dropped, so the longer you can leave any decisions and the more you can talk things through, the more likely you are to come out the other end with a decision that's better than purely running on emotion. Looking back on it, I was better off for the process of talking to Gilbert, to Kelly, and to my family. At that stage, apart from the text from Braces, I didn't hear from anyone on the selection panel or anyone from New Zealand Cricket.

About two weeks later I went back to Canterbury. Going into the Canterbury squad was not exactly an embarrassment, but it was certainly a new feeling, walking into the first training, having played for so long for the national team and then being dropped. You've got to accept it as part of what you do, but I was nervous going back in. You wonder what the other players are thinking. You start to wonder if you're too old.

But going back to play for Canterbury, I found that everyone there, the guys in the team and Dave Molesworthy the coach, were all fantastic as far as accepting me as a cricketer. Basically, nothing was said about me having been dropped from the Black Caps, which was good, because the state that I was in, the more I talked about it, the more pissed off I was likely to get.

They just got me back into the team and got me to play cricket. The first couple of games I played, my scores were awful, because mentally I was still in a bad space. I ended up doing some basic work with Dave, and then got some good runs for Canterbury.

For a while I was still annoyed, still unhappy, but before long I reached a stage where it was just, 'Bugger it, I don't care what you guys do with the New Zealand team. I've been there, I've played enough cricket, I've had a reasonable career, so now I'm just going to go out and enjoy my cricket.' I think that was probably the turning point for me. I wasn't trying too hard, I got back to just going out and watching the ball, and then it was a case of see the ball, hit the ball.

To put it in blunt terms, I didn't give a rat's arse any more. It was about enjoying the game, and whatever happened would happen: selection was out of my control. Things did pick up, and so I guess the selectors would say, 'Well, it worked'. It was a big moment in my life, certainly in my cricketing life, and maybe I did get a bit more of my enjoyment back, and that might have been missing.

Did I ever feel that I was showing the selectors how wrong they were? Trying to embarrass them about dropping me? No. When you're in a bad patch of form, negative emotion is the worst thing for you. You're thinking about a whole bunch of things you should be doing, rather than just watching the cricket ball. If I went out and thought, 'Right, I'm going to show you that you were wrong', then I'd just tense up and wouldn't achieve what I wanted. In contrast, if I just went out and thought 'Bugger it, I'll play the way I want to play', it felt like a weight off my shoulders and I started to get some runs again.

I can't say enough about the fact that, not just with me, but with any cricketer, you'll play better if you're thinking about just one thing, not a whole range of issues, some of them off the pitch.

My recall into the Black Caps squad came purely out of luck. My mate Mr Fleming was becoming a father at that time, and there was a need for another batsman.

Stephen Fleming: You've go to understand, I was doing everything I could to keep him in the side. I had a tumour on my face, and then Kelly had our first child, Taylor, so I kept texting him saying, 'Look, I'm doing everything I can buddy'.

New Zealand was playing Sri Lanka in Queenstown on the Saturday. I was at my sister's house when I got a call saying that Flem was out and I was wanted to cover for the squad. There was a game for Canterbury on the Friday, and they wanted me to stay and play in that. That was fine.

On the morning of the game I caught the 6 a.m. flight to Queenstown. I'd been told I was coming down to cover and that Peter Fulton was going to play. I got down there, went into the hotel, and then walked down the steps to take the early bus to the hotel with the others who weren't playing. Braces had just got off the phone. He said, 'I just phoned you, and left a message on your phone to say you're playing. You're the super sub.'

That was all news to me and I was annoyed. I knew for a fact that the night before they had had a team meeting and the team is always named that night. So, after a bit of investigation, talking to a few guys, it became clear that I'd been named as the super sub the night before. It was only a little thing, but it really annoyed me.

I felt that I should have been called so that I knew I was playing and could have been properly prepared. Rather than leaving me feeling that I was down there to cover, maybe to have a bit of fun.

It was an example of a needless communication breakdown: one phone call would have given me a heads-up. You prepare differently if you know you're playing the game.

So I played, got two, and then we came back up to Christchurch. Flem was still out, and I played and scored 90. After the game, I was pulled aside in the changing shed and told that I wouldn't be required for the rest of the series. Braces took me aside, and rather than just saying, 'Okay Nathan, you're not selected, Stephen's coming back, that was always the plan', which I could have handled better, he got nervous, or clouded — I'm not too sure — but it got to the point where he was saying, 'I know that it is affecting you financially, and it's not a nice thing to go through'. There were other bits and pieces that he was also saying, rather than just, 'Stephen's back, you're not in the team', which, for me, would have been the end of it. It was also mentioned that they wanted to carry on trying out the younger guys, because, I think, at that stage we were up 3–0 in the series. I was pretty peeved about that, too.

Cricinfo, January 6, 2006:

Nathan Astle, dropped from the New Zealand squad for the remaining two matches of a five-match series against Sri Lanka, was told that the controversial move was in keeping with the side's 'long-term planning'. Astle returned from a prolonged batting slump to score a match-winning unbeaten 90 in New Zealand's five-wicket win over Sri Lanka in Christchurch on Tuesday, but was dropped to accommodate Stephen Fleming, who returned from paternal leave for the last two matches of the series.

John Bracewell, New Zealand's coach, defended his stance on

Astle by saying that the side needed to expand its depth and build competition within the ranks as preparation for the World Cup in 2007. Bracewell's announcement generated much criticism given that Hamish Marshall, also in a slump, was retained despite scoring just 12 in the last match.

Bracewell's justification for this was that Marshall was a middle-order batsman and that Astle was replaced by a top-order batsman. Marshall has been the worst-performing batsman in the squad for nearly a year, but Bracewell said neither his run-drought nor Astle's revival justified a change in plan.

'I was quite clear with Nathan last [Tuesday] night, which isn't the easiest thing to do when a guy comes off in that position, to give him that sort of news,' he told the *New Zealand Herald* today. 'But we've got to understand that we need to develop depth within our cricket to be competitive. That's pretty difficult to understand if you're the individual affected.'

Bracewell conceded that he and Astle weren't necessarily seeing eye-to-eye on the subject. 'It was tough for him. He accepted it. I'm not quite sure if he really understands it yet,' he added. 'But if you look back at anybody in that situation, they don't necessarily have the understanding, or even the desire to understand.'

On Astle's series-winning knock at Jade Stadium, Bracewell admitted it was a good sign. 'I don't think he batted with particular fluency but he delivered the character that we were wanting; the sort of character you get from a guy who digs that little bit deeper when they're not in form,' he said. 'There was effort. There was a ton of stickability and grit, which is something else that you need within your players. You've got to admire that.'

The last game was in Napier and there was an injury cloud over, I think, Scott Styris. Once again, I was called up. This is where things started to get a bit cloudy for me. The selectors had said that they wanted me to go away and get runs, which was fine, and I had. But then they kept saying that they wanted to try the younger guys, to give them a crack at international level. So which was it?

It was probably a fair call to try out some of the new guys as we were up 3–0 in the series by then and the last game was a fine time to do it. So I was going up to cover for Scott Styris. I ended up playing the game ahead of Jamie How, and I remember saying to him, 'This is bullshit. You should be playing this game ahead of me.' It was a good time to try someone like him.

The selectors' argument was that they wanted me in the team to cover a bowling option, which I still think is something they hid behind. Whether that's the case or not, I don't know. But I bowled just three overs in the game. To me, it was still a golden opportunity to play Jamie How ahead of me.

I have no real idea as to why it was going on. That was when I started to think, not that there was a conspiracy, but there was more behind the dropping than I was aware of. Some bigger policy that wasn't out in the open.

Throughout the whole series, I felt that Braces didn't have a lot to say to me after I'd got back in the team. It wasn't as if we hated each other, not at all, but there was a coldness there. It was hard to sit next to him or be in a room with no one else around. It was uncomfortable.

Then the West Indies arrived. I was in the squad from the start and went through the whole series. Things improved a little, but there was still an undercurrent of something not being right. I was starting to hear rumours of Ric Charlesworth coming into the management structure, which made the older guys feel uncomfortable and the younger guys more comfortable.

There was another phone call with Braces. I rang him, and I was still pissed off I guess, and pointed out that there were other guys in the team in the same boat as me, not scoring as many runs as they'd like, if not worse. The response was, 'We wanted to give you a kick up the arse: whether it was because you'd got comfortable, or your life had moved on and you've got a family now'. I can remember thinking, 'I don't think my family life has got anything to do with what you think. You're making assumptions.'

That was when I started to put two and two together regarding Ric Charlesworth — an Australian who had become New Zealand Cricket's high-performance manager just two months before. He had played State cricket for Western Australia, hockey for Australia, and had coached the Australian women's hockey team to two Olympic gold medals. In Australia, he'd won national awards as a coach, and had been the author of several books on coaching. One of the coaching concepts he'd written about was to keep senior players unsettled, so they wouldn't become complacent.

It seemed to me that perhaps I was being used as an example of a senior player who had been in the Black Caps for a long time getting a kick up the bum. I guess, looking at the results against Sri Lanka and the West Indies, you'd have to say it worked.

Conversations with other older guys in the team, who I'm reluctant to name, revealed that there was some heat on them as well. Not to the point of being dropped, but things were being said to them. My gut feeling is that senior guys were being targeted because they thought we were getting comfortable. I don't believe that anyone in the team thought it was a God-given right to be there. Maybe in the past guys might have played for themselves. But in the culture that I knew, it wasn't the case.

I think there was an uncomfortable feeling in the whole squad. A lot of guys saw a different direction in the team after Ric Charlesworth arrived. It's my opinion — and it's only an opinion — that even Flem found it uncomfortable. When Flem came back into the team he was told that they couldn't say whether or not he'd be captain for the next three games, as Dan Vettori was doing such a good job. Saying that to someone who's been doing the job since he was 24, and done it so well for us, seemed very odd to me. Of course, I was aware that there was much I didn't know, including how much pressure Braces was copping, and whether he'd agreed with it, or had had to do it.

John Bracewell: I don't think he's incorrect in seeing a change, but I do think the paranoia is a little strong. With any change in personnel, and especially with somebody as strong, and with as strong a reputation as Ric has, in terms of developing teams, you are going to get change. He was actually brought in to change the New Zealand high-performance programme.

Immediately you're going to get a bit of, 'Ooh, what's going on here?'. That ignites the flame, and once you get a group of senior players who feel a little bit uncomfortable with change, because they've ruled the roost for so long, that's always going to fuel the fire. But I don't think there's any shame in investigating change if New Zealand want to be the best in the world. It was as uncomfortable a time for me as it was for the players.

But out of it I believe we've emerged a stronger unit. We've emerged recognising that to be the best in the world we have to make changes ourselves. Nathan's been part of that with our leadership group, helping to initiate changes. But the first step is always the scariest one. It's a case of 'How cold IS that water?'.

I have a different approach to Ric. I certainly agree with a number of things he wants to put in place, but I also disagree with some things he wants. That's healthy. He has a great depth of experience I want to use as a resource, but I will make my own decisions. In the end any decision made about the Black Caps, with selection, for example, is something I'm accountable for.

So I wouldn't offload anything on anyone else. I get ideas from all sorts of places. From books, from other people, from teams, from sitting down for four hours in Hamilton with [Sri Lankan coach] Tom Moody about how he's developing his side. I'll try to work them into our culture, if I think they're worthwhile.

Stephen Fleming: I knew there were some things going on. I knew that the selectors wanted to make some of the senior players uncomfortable, from my captaincy through to the players. My captaincy had been questioned in the media by Braces, so I knew what was happening there.

I thought I had a read on it when they put Nathan under pressure, but when he responded with runs I couldn't understand why his place was still under pressure, I thought making the runs was enough. What I couldn't understand, and what was never really measured, was the emotional strain on a player, especially a player who has played a bit, and is coming towards the end of his career.

The emotional strain that was put on Nathan and Chris Cairns was never measured. These guys were working under unbelievable pressure to perform during a game with the axe hanging over them. So while Nathan was busting his gut, and Chris Cairns the same, perhaps when these guys came back, the prize for getting back was just not quite as golden as it had been when they were younger and first had a taste of it. All of a sudden, the thrill of playing international cricket and travelling was not quite a good enough reward for the stresses and the amount of strain they were being put through at that time.

I've always wondered, looking back at it, whether that time forced the retirement of Chris and then the retirement of Nathan. You can never measure how much emotional strain it puts on your family, or on Nathan. The three things he cited as the main reasons for retiring was that he wanted more time with his family, he was emotionally spent, and he wasn't enjoying it any more.

Those were the sort of things imposed on him by the selectors' course during his time out of the team. Professionally, you can see what they were doing, but you have to be very careful about the individual, and the character of the person you're doing it to, and I'm still not sure that they got the best result out of that.

The West Indies series in February 2006 found me at a stage where I didn't care about the selectors' attitude to me. I had a good series, and while I was still uncomfortable around Braces, Ric Charlesworth and the selectors, I was in a space where I just went out and played my game, and the results were better for that approach.

As I've mentioned above, the selectors could therefore say that their approach worked, and that's fair enough. But I didn't like the way that it was done. It may sound a bit soft, but I think that after what I'd given to New Zealand cricket over the years, I deserved a better explanation than what I finally received.

What made it ironic was that I ended up going to the national awards and winning the Player of the Year award for batting — even after such an unsettled year. The biggest thing as far as the dropping went was that I'd had a very good tour of Zimbabwe beforehand, but missed out in the one-day games in South Africa, and then didn't get big scores against Aussie. But it wasn't as if it was a long series of poor form. There were about six innings that were scratchy, and then I was dropped.

We all had an end-of-year review — where we sit down with Lindsay Crocker, John Bracewell, and, usually, Warren Frost, our fitness adviser, to review our whole year. It was really the only chance I'd had until then to talk about what was going on with me. At that stage, I was still in a bad space with Braces and the selectors.

Usually Gilbert Enoka is also there, but when I got to this meeting he wasn't. There were a few things I wanted to get off my chest, and I wanted him there, not so much as a backup for me, but to facilitate the discussion, rather than letting it get to a situation where I'd be getting hammered by them when I was by myself.

The first thing I said was that I wasn't happy about sitting down and doing it, because I'd understood Gilbert was going to be there. They ummed and aahed, and finally we reached an understanding that we'd just review the cricket side of things.

They have a list of different categories from batting and bowling to skill work, and the marks run from one to five, with five being the highest. We went through the first couple of categories and I think my highest score was two. I thought, 'Mmmm. Okay.'

Every time there was a mark, Braces would ask, 'What do you think of that?'. I'd give my opinion. 'Well, I think my catching is pretty good. I think I deserve more than that.' We'd done about four or five of these, and it got to a stage where it seemed to me that Warren, our fitness guy, could see it was getting to a point where I was peed off. He jumped in and said, 'Braces, when you ask Nathan what he thinks, does what he says have any relevance to the marks? Is it going to move you on what you think as far as the marks go?' Braces said, 'No'.

This got my back up, and I said, 'I've got no interest in carrying this on. You're not listening to what I'm saying. You're giving me these marks, which is fine, but when I disagree with them, we're not coming to any median ground on these.'

They said they saw my season as one of two halves. Obviously, Zimbabwe and South Africa was the first half, and the rest of the summer the second. I said, 'Well, you say there were two halves. What if I were to say to you that there were six one-day internationals in which I performed poorly. You can't say to me that I was poor in Zimbabwe, or against Sri Lanka, or against the West Indies. You're telling me those six one-day games make up half the year. That's just not true. That's not right.'

They gave reviews of tours as well, and Braces had given me a good review of the South African tour. In his view, even though as far as the cricket went it hadn't been flash for me, he felt that what I gave to the team as a senior player was very good.

But I wasn't really comfortable with that. To me it felt like a case of trying to give me something to make me feel happier about what had happened over the whole summer.

Braces finished doing the sheet, and then they said, 'Is there anything else you'd like to talk about?'. I said there was, but I wasn't prepared to do it in this sort of forum. That was pretty much where it was left. I don't think I even said goodbye to Braces.

John Bracewell: Our normal review process is done with Gilbert Enoka there, but because of what we'd gone through there was almost a Mexican stand-off between us.

I think the messages that had gone out to Nathan, the understanding of those messages, and perhaps even the poor communication of those messages, without poking the borax at anyone in particular, meant that the need for Gilbert to be there as a facilitator was vital. And, of course, he wasn't there.

So it was an extremely strained meeting. We got about three-quarters of the way through it, and we stopped because it became so obviously strained. Sometimes you need to pull the pin and redo it. It was a meeting going nowhere as a review process. It was just becoming more and more strained, and we were always going to agree to disagree.

It was a tough time for both of us. It was tough for me because: one, he was still an important part of my plan; two, I realised my communication had been poor during that period with him; and three, his stubbornness to accept that it wasn't personalised.

There is no way that it was ever a personal attack on Nathan, because I had the utmost respect for him as a cricketer, and as an ethical man, and as a friend within the side. There are few players of whom you'd say, 'I would like to be friends with this guy'. As a coach you have to be detached, because at times you have to be the judge and executioner. But he is a guy that I really liked.

I don't think Nathan was able to fit 'like' and 'selection' into the same sort of category. I think there was a bit of, 'Well, if he likes me, why isn't he picking me?'.

Because he's the type of bloke he is, he really struggled with it. But I didn't struggle with it in the same way, because I know that I have to make those decisions. It's the same with Hamish Marshall. He has all the attributes that you want in a player in your team. But he's just got to get some runs. That's the bottom line.

Lindsay Crocker followed me out — I guess because he could see that I was pretty annoyed — and I went down to his office. I said, 'Mate, that is just the biggest load of rubbish I've ever listened to. I walked out of there, and I feel that I'm not going to be able to carry on playing with Braces giving me that sort of feedback. I don't think it's fair.'

Lindsay was good. He talked me through it until I'd calmed

down again, and we left it at that. I came home, had about six weeks off, and then I went to England to play for Lancashire. I didn't hear from anyone from New Zealand Cricket once in all of that time.

Then I got an email to say that I was in the ICC Champions Trophy one-day tournament squad of 30 to go to India, so that was okay. I came back from England, had two days at home, and then we had a camp with the whole squad out at Lincoln.

They'd got a guy from Australia to try to take the leadership group further, which was fine. Part of this was peer review sessions where one player would go outside the room, and those left would split into groups to come up with three words to say how you'd describe him — like stubborn, that sort of stuff — as well as three things he should start doing and three things he should stop doing. The person outside the room has to come up with what he thinks the group perception of him is.

So the person comes back in and sits out the front, and then one person from each group tells them what they thought. Braces did his, and he wrote down as a possible group perception of himself, 'dishonest', which I think may have been connected with other guys that had been dropped like myself, and with what they'd been told.

We were just sitting there, and for some reason Richard Hadlee, who was one of the selectors, came and sat down next to me. He asked how I was going. I replied, and then he asked how Braces and I were getting on.

I said, 'Yeah, I think sort of so-so'.

Then he said, 'Just out of interest, can you tell me what you were told last year when you got dropped?'.

That caught me by surprise. I said, 'I was told I had to go back and get runs at first-class level and you guys wanted to try some younger players. That's what I was told.'

He looked at me and said, 'Really? That wasn't the message you were meant to get.'

Away from the cricket pitch, you'll usually find Nathan has a golf club in his hands.

New Year's Eve at the Rakaia huts outside Christchurch, and you can see how alcohol doesn't unlock the inhibitions of Gary Stead, Nathan and Geoff Allott!

Not entirely typical of Nathan's room on tour: the bats aren't perfectly lined up, and some gear hasn't been tidied away.

Above: In India, where cricket fans are the keenest in the world, it's easy to persuade security guards to share time, and weapons, for a photo.

Left: 'Elvis' Astle, possibly ready to leave the building, at a celebration in Australia.

While Flem directs, Nathan works on one last fingernail.

The aggression in Nathan's pull shot, with the front foot off the ground and out of the way, is demonstrated in the third one-day game against India at Jade Stadium in 2003, as he smashed his way to 32 off 20 balls. New Zealand won by five wickets.

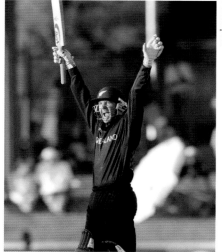

One of the golden memories for Nathan. Stephen Fleming salutes the crowd after scoring 134 in a 2003 World Cup game against South Africa. Nathan finished on 54, and the game was won by nine wickets.

So happy it looks like he raised two bats. Nathan celebrates a century in Bloemfontein against Zimbabwe at the 2003 World Cup. He was not out on 102, and the Black Caps won by six wickets.

Nathan contemplates a test dismissal at Jade Stadium: not happy, and not so much spitting the dummy, as, more typically for him, chewing the chin strap.

The woman who brought out the romantic side of Nathan Astle —
his wife Kelly.

The pleasures of more time at home after leaving the Black Caps. Nathan and Kelly at home with Liam (left) and Alyssa.

I was startled. I said, 'Well, what was I meant to get?'.

He said, 'As a selection panel we felt your game had become static, and the game was passing you by'.

Looking back on it, as I mentioned before, because my form wasn't great, perhaps I had been training too hard, and trying too hard, and not playing the way I should have been playing, for myself and for the team.

Richard said, 'We felt the game was moving on, and you do a good job getting us off to a good start. All the way through the middle you accumulate your singles, and then you go again at the end. We felt that you obviously had a bit of bad form, and your game was being left behind, because in the game these days you need more through the middle period.'

I thought it was a fair point.

'So what we wanted you to do was to go back, get some runs, and try to develop your game a bit more into that sort of style.'

I said to Paddles, 'That's fine, but it wasn't what I got told. To be perfectly honest, isn't it the coach's job, if that's what he's feeling, to get hold of me when he first thought of this problem, to get hold of me then, rather than later? To pull me aside, to tell me what they want from me?'

He agreed with me. I thanked Richard for coming up to me and giving me that message.

I think if I'd been told that from the outset, and had also been made aware of the fact that they might want to use some younger guys, that I would have been a lot more at ease and accepted being dropped a lot better than I did. It may be a little thing, but whether Braces was nervous or got mixed up in delivering the message, I don't know.

It was bloody good on Richard's part, because obviously he'd heard that something wasn't right. He went on to say that even after the century against the West Indies it was still a bit of a struggle to keep me in the team. I asked him why that was.

He said that, again, they felt I could have starting upping the run rate earlier against the West Indies, that my game hadn't moved on as much as they wanted.

I said, 'Richard, I got 130. We won the game.'

He said, 'But you hit three sixes off the last three balls'.

'Okay, but I think if you go back and look at the game situation, we were losing wickets quite regularly, so now you're telling me to go and have a go, but if I get out I'm stuffed anyway. I'm damned if I do and damned if I don't. You can't say that to a player. The fact is that I got 130, we won the game.'

I added, 'We were losing wickets. I'd like to think that my experience helped me read the situation, and I thought that I had to bat a longer period.' I think he accepted that. I did find it interesting, though, that after that game there was still discussion about whether I should be in the team, and they were still unhappy.

That was the end of that, but then I thought, 'I've got to go and sit down with Braces, and talk the whole thing out with him'. I said that I wanted to have a yarn with him about what had happened over the last year and the messages I'd been getting.

To be fair to him, he was bloody good. First of all, I said that I personally felt uncomfortable around him, and that our relationship wasn't the same as it had been when he first took over coaching the team. It had gone downhill big time.

I said, 'Even after a winter of not seeing each other, I think there are still undercurrents as a result of what's been going on'.

He said, 'Do you really think that?'.

I said, 'Yes, I do'.

'I thought there was a little bit,' he said, 'but I didn't think it was too bad.'

Then I just told him how I'd seen what had happened the previous season, what Richard had told me, and I said, 'From a coaching point of view, I know that I'm a senior guy, but there are times when you need to come and tell me if you think I need to be working on something else'.

He accepted that, and we pretty much left the fact that communications over the summer — whether between him and me, me and the selectors, or whoever it was — were poor.

I said to him, 'The most disappointing thing to me was that it got to that stage. Perhaps I should have come to you earlier, or you should have come to me. It festered and I probably got bitter, as a lot of stuff happened that could have been knocked on the head six months earlier.'

I'm not a confrontational guy, but if something does need to be said I will say it. The guy they brought in from Australia probably did prick me into doing something about it. Otherwise, it would have got worse, which wouldn't have been good for me or the team.

Braces is a very strong-headed man, and for him to accept that some of what he did was wrong was good to hear. There were parts that I probably could have been better at as well.

Steve Rixon: The process with a player has to be about winning his trust. Once you've got his trust, you can talk like two normal human beings, and therefore you can get an answer. If you have two people talking without any shields up, it'll work. If one person is dictating, it won't work.

You don't put obstacles in the way as a coach, you don't mix the messages, rather, you keep everything open and free, so people know where they stand.

Glenn Turner (New Zealand selector): Up until the last few years, getting a hundred off 120 balls would most often win a game. More recently that was not necessarily the case, because under good conditions sides can get 300-plus.

Therefore, with 300 balls in an innings, your strike rate

often has to be over 100, so how we wanted to encourage Nathan to change was to say, 'Hey Nathan, what you're doing at the moment is that while you often still get away to a rollicking start, in those middle stages, where it's as though you're starting to slow right down, you seem to be saying to yourself, "Right, I've got to establish myself here. I'll hold the innings together, the innings will build around me, and therefore all I need to do is just tick [the score] over."'

We're saying, 'Don't do that, keep on being aggressive, keep looking to attack first, defend second, because your hundred has to come off 90 balls, rather than 120'.

I recall one specific instance where Hamish Marshall, who's not really a boundary hitter, slogged out, while Nathan at the other end, on 80 or 90, was taking ones, but it was Hamish who tried to launch it over the top. I thought, 'Hell, Nathan's far better equipped to do that'.

I recall Paddles coming back to a selection meeting, and saying that Nathan hadn't been told [to change the pacing of his innings]. I can confirm that. The thing that frustrated me, towards the end, was that Nathan had the skills to do that and probably only needed to be told.

John Bracewell: The messages that Nathan got for why he was out may have been blurred, and the communication of that message was probably poor and that's my fault. I'm in charge of that, and if he didn't get that message clearly enough, then I'm the one who's responsible.

One thing about Nathan is that he's not a dishonest man. He doesn't tell lies. He doesn't exaggerate and he doesn't try to say things to prove he's right or wrong. So I would say that undoubtedly my communication with him must have been poor.

Answering the Burning Question

You don't make a decision lightly to give up something that has been your work, your life, and your passion for more than a decade. My decision to retire from international cricket after our one-day win over England in Adelaide in January, all started, I believe, 15 months earlier, when I was dropped from the Black Caps.

From then on — from when I got back into the team permanently against the West Indies in February 2006 — for some reason the enjoyment just wasn't there, even though we were doing well and I was scoring runs.

I just couldn't find the satisfaction that had always been there in the past when the team was doing well, and I was doing well. That was when I started to think, 'Hang on, this is not quite right'.

I think it was always sitting in the back of my mind the whole way through, and it'd pop up more when I wasn't doing well, which is human nature. Every time I thought of it, I'd go down the track of saying, 'Right, go to the World Cup in the West Indies, and then it's all done and dusted'. Perhaps that was my way of coping with a decision everyone in sport finds hard to make.

Before we went to Australia I'd mentioned the possibility of retiring to Kelly, but really not much more than just a mention. It was mostly me dealing with it. In the weeks before we went I was very close to ringing Braces and saying that I didn't want to go. But I thought I should try one more time. Time would prove that it wasn't to be.

I guess I was trying to persuade myself that it would be okay. In the process I probably talked up how good I was feeling about the game not only to myself, but to other people as well. One thing I've always said to Kelly was that as long as I was enjoying the game, I'd keep playing at that level. But as soon as the enjoyment wasn't there, I was gone. And eventually that caught up to me.

In the games against Sri Lanka I did alright in one, but not in the other — and then my performances against Aussie were awful. Every second day in Australia, I'd think about retirement. It'd just pop into my head, or I'd think about the kids back home, which was not the major reason for my retirement, but was certainly a big part of it.

I rang Gilbert Enoka a week before we went to Perth and said, 'Look mate, it's just not happening for me any more, I don't want to be here. There's no enjoyment, the motivation has gone, everything's just a hassle.'

To me I never think of Bert in his official role as the Black Caps mental skills coach, he's much more of a mate, who I've got to know really well over the years. If I want to talk to him about anything in life, not just cricket, I can do that. He's been around the traps for a while, and had a lot to do with international sportspeople, so I think he's got a fair insight into how we work.

He said to think more about it. I did that for about three or four days, then I rang him back, two days out from the Adelaide game, to say that it was over. First of all, he said, he needed 24 hours to think about it himself, and we'd go from there; so, of course, I let him have that time.

He rang back the next day, and asked if anything had changed. I said, 'No, it hasn't'. He said, 'Well then, I think you're probably right, it is time for you to go'.

That was the lead-in to it. Before it was announced, I talked with Kelly, and with my family — not so much looking for advice, but more running it past them to make sure it wasn't a rash decision.

When I walked out to bat in Adelaide I was the only person in the New Zealand camp who knew it was my last game. Actually, I was the only one, full stop. Even Kelly and my family didn't know for sure that it was over.

After the game, I rang Kelly and said to her, 'That's it. I'm finished.'

I'd slept well the night before the game, because I knew the decision was made, and I was playing, so that occupied me too.

In the last moment of the game I took a catch that finished the English innings. Some might say it was the happiest I'd looked on tour, perhaps the first time I'd looked happy on the field at all. My body language must have been telling some stories. When I told my dad I was retiring he said, 'Look, it doesn't surprise me'. He knows me so well that he'd been picking up the vibes over the last little while. There was just no motivation there any more. Standing in the field for 50 overs was starting to feel like 300.

The way I've played my cricket has always been pretty basic. I train what I think I need to train. But now there's lots of extra stuff —meetings, analysing games and so on — the sorts of things I've never really agreed with. I've given some things a fair crack, but found that, for me, it overcomplicated things and just made it harder, because it's not really me.

A criticism some of the other players, even Flem, had of me

was that I didn't give enough to the team in those situations, but basically I just didn't agree with what was being done, but I was happy enough to go along with it because there were other guys who might benefit from it.

Mind you, if there is something to say I'll certainly say it. That was something I perhaps did bring to the meetings. If I spoke up people would go, 'Hang on, he must really mean this because he's saying something'.

Cricket's never going to be an exact science, there are just so many things that can happen in a day, for some funny, unexplained reason. So to sit down and go through everything that doesn't go right on the day and then try to find an explanation for it, will always, I believe, be a mission impossible.

Sure, there are some things you can work on, like catching, or if you're regularly getting out the same way then obviously there's something there to be looked at. Otherwise I don't think it's worthwhile.

John Bracewell: In 2006 I had sat down with Nathan, with a number of the leadership group, and a few who I regarded as the vital few for the World Cup. I explained to each one what I saw as his particular role at the World Cup.

I put Nathan and Stephen [Fleming] in exactly the same bracket. I said that, 'You've been to several World Cups, so this is not your time for being the men who win it . . . but we need your experience, we need you as mentors'.

It was vital that we had that sort of experience on the bus to make up that combination. Nathan's retirement threw a bit of a cog in the works of my makeup of the squad for the World Cup. You need that balance, that perfect team balance, right the way through. Nathan and Stephen were vital parts of that.

The night after the game in which we beat England in Adelaide [Tuesday, 23 January 2007], a few of the guys went out. I just stayed in my room, and I think I got one or two hours' sleep that whole night, because I knew what was coming the next day. The burning question still going through my mind was, of course, whether I was doing the right thing. But although I got hardly any sleep, it was still the best night I'd had on tour. I just lay there thinking about everything that I'd done, what had been going through my mind over the past year or so, and by the time I'd finished I was set in my mind about what I was going to do.

On the Wednesday morning in Adelaide, I spoke first to Bert [Enoka], who wanted to run through things just once more, then I rang Kelly, and then my parents. At the airport I spoke with Flem and told him. I think he was surprised but not totally surprised.

Like a lot of people, he sort of knew it was coming, although he probably didn't expect it to be as early. He was very good. He didn't try to talk me out of it, because he knew it was not the sort of thing I'd do on a whim. I appreciated that.

Stephen Fleming: I knew from past experience, with Chris Cairns in particular, that when Nathan said, 'Mate, I'm done', that even to say, 'Are you sure?' would be almost a slap in the face for a guy who is so sincere, who was making a statement like that.

To me, he was gone. He wouldn't make that decision lightly. He's not the sort of person who was really looking for a pat on the back, to be told, 'Come on mate, we'll get through this week first', or stuff like that. It's not what makes him tick.

He was never one to have emotional banners strewn around everywhere. Always straight up, never any grandstanding. He never tried to use the emotional side of things to his advantage.

He was always sincere in his emotions towards the game and the team.

For him to say he was gone, my first reaction was to accept it straight away. Then I found that I wasn't ready to accept it for my own closure, but I knew that Nathan had made a decision that was selfless. I knew he'd get some criticism for the timing, but I couldn't see it as being anything other than selfless, knowing that the World Cup was coming, just around the corner really, three months away.

I thought it was an incredibly professional and fair decision to give Lou [Vincent] time to adjust to being in the team before the World Cup.

When we got to Perth and were in the hotel, I went with Flem to see [New Zealand Cricket Chief Executive] Martin Snedden. He was very good too. Martin drew some parallels with the new job he's got with the 2011 Rugby World Cup organisation. He said how he had found it hard to make that decision, but once he knew he had a finite date to leave New Zealand Cricket, he could feel a huge weight lift off his shoulders and he could work to the date.

Obviously, he was suggesting that the World Cup might be that date for me. He said if I did that, knowing I was going at the end of the World Cup, I might find some more enjoyment there and keep playing. It was fair reasoning, and I did listen and take it in. But it wasn't enough to change my mind. He was very fair, and we got Lindsay Crocker [the team manager] and John Bracewell together.

Sneds and Flem had broken the news to them. They asked if there was anything they could do to keep me playing. They offered to send me home, to allow me to just get away from it for a bit, and have me come back for the Chappell-Hadlee series. I said no, that I appreciated it, but it wouldn't change my mind.

Braces was very surprised. On the way back from the Champions Trophy in India in October 2006 we'd had breakfast, and he'd asked me how I was travelling, and I'd said that I was enjoying it. Was that some sort of white lie? Perhaps, but is it a white lie if you've persuaded yourself to believe it? And there were days over that time when it was fine, but unfortunately, they became fewer and further between.

I just couldn't find the motivation you need to go to the meetings, go to the gym, go to training. You have to have that to get any benefit from it all.

John Bracewell: On the one hand, I'd done a lot of planning about Nathan, getting him in the right state of mind, getting his energy levels up, getting him to help to mentor, because although he's a reluctant leader he's someone that young people gravitate to for quiet advice.

He's not a guy with a great repartee when talking to a group, but I've actually used him on tour as what we call a critical friend. He's a guy that I went to and said, 'Through this tour I'd like you to give me advice about how I'm travelling', and he was outstanding on a one-to-one basis. So in that, I felt slightly let down; we'd be missing the contribution he could have made.

On the other hand, there's the courage he showed, because it would have been easy to take a pay cheque through to the World Cup. Without a job in the wings, he could have cruised his way through. So the selflessness, I think, has to be admired. He gave Lou an opportunity to bed in. Lou was hitting form at the time, and although I don't think that had any influence on Nathan's decision, the transition from him to Lou was actually quite smooth.

We lack the experience now, but we've got a cricketer

of such ability he has seamlessly moved into the position Nathan held. That was a stroke of luck really. But it was selfless of Nathan to not take a cheque to the end of the World Cup and then find a job he wanted. Instead, he decided he wasn't enjoying it, that it was time to move on, and you've got to admire that.

Stephen Fleming: (Laughing.) Believe me, money does matter to Nath. When the players heard it they knew it was a serious decision if he was giving up cash. Hell, I reckon giving up his meal allowance for that part of our time in Perth would have hurt.

John Bracewell: Was Nathan ever in danger of being dropped before the World Cup? No. There was no doubt in my mind that Nathan's form, like Stephen's form, would return. People didn't really understand either that in the early section of the Tri-Series in Australia we were playing on some pretty difficult wickets, and, in fact, had been playing on poor tracks for quite some time. In South Africa, we played on some minefields; there were poor tracks at the ICC tournament in India; we had a poor summer in New Zealand where there were seaming wickets; and when we went to Australia, the wickets were pretty indifferent, until we got to Perth.

Nathan's form had been reasonably consistent. He's always been a feast or famine cricketer, he's not one who gets a lot of 30s and 40s. He gets a big one, or he gets next to nothing. He got a 45 in Hobart on a flat deck, top scoring in an innings of 205, batting bloody well, which would equate to a 70 or an 80 on a better wicket. So I didn't have major concerns with Nathan's form, the way he was training, the way he was practising, which is probably why it was such a shock when he retired.

When Martin Snedden knocked on my door in Perth and said, 'I need to see you', I thought, 'Shit, here we go'. I thought it was about me. (Laughs.) So he came and sat down and told me, 'Nathan's just come to see me with Stephen Fleming, and he's retiring. I've just spent three-quarters of an hour with him.' So he told Martin before he told anyone else. Stephen told me that he didn't know until the day we went to Perth.

Why didn't I announce my retirement in Adelaide? I thought about it, but there really wasn't time. We left Adelaide very early on a Wednesday morning. I knew that when we got to Perth the next game wasn't until the Sunday. I know that it was a long way to travel to make the announcement, but in Perth there would be time to sit down, talk it through, have the press conference, to do everything that needed to be done.

Because we were leaving in the morning, I firmly believe that if I'd told team management in Adelaide, they would have insisted I go to Perth and have the press conference. I doubt they would have wanted me to just jump on a plane and come home from Adelaide — if you were a conspiracy theorist, that would have created even more of an uproar. And then there was also the fact that we'd just won a game, and it just didn't feel right to go straight away.

Was the timing of my retirement wrong? Maybe, but there's never an ideal time to say you're leaving. Some people have asked why I didn't go through to the end of the tour. Perhaps I could have got through. But that wouldn't have been fair on my team-mates.

In the state of mind I was in, I really felt it was better to bring someone in who wanted to be there, who would go through to the

World Cup, who was playing for all the right reasons, so he could get a bit of a lead-in to the World Cup with some top cricket under his belt.

I have a lot of respect for Flem, he's my best mate, and I especially thought it wouldn't be fair on him to keep going. That helped sway me to do it there and then. If I'd gone to the end of the series and then called it quits, I wouldn't have blamed people in my environment, in the team, for being pissed off with me.

I did get the chance to talk with most of the guys in Perth, one-on-one. I tried to explain to them why I was doing it, and answered any questions they had. Brendon McCullum is someone I get on very well with. He was very open. He said he didn't agree with it, but he fully understood and supported what I'd done.

I've become quite good friends with Travis Wilson, our fielding coach, who's an upfront sort of guy. He just said, 'Mate, why are you doing this?'. When you hear your mates say that, it makes it a bit harder, but I think after we'd talked they all understood my reasons.

There must have been guys who just thought it was bad timing, and a lot were pretty shocked, but I think once they'd digested it, they understood. I hope that was the case anyway. If I'd had to sit in front of the whole team and tell them, it would have been so overwhelming that I might have burst into tears. For me, the way to do it was individually.

On the Wednesday night, our first in Perth, a group of us went out to dinner: Flem, Dan Vettori and Brendon. That was when I told Dan and Brendon. I'd got round pretty much all the guys before we went out. It was a good way to sign off with them.

John Bracewell: After Martin [Snedden] and I talked [in Perth] we met with Lindsay Crocker, and then we had to work out the implications of what Nathan had told us.

The A plan, B plan, sort of stuff.

Nathan and Stephen came in, and we told them what we thought was the A plan. How could we help you through this? Could we bring Kelly and the kids over? What would assist you, not to change your mind altogether, but to get you through to the World Cup, so you've got peace of mind, and feel happy to be playing cricket in the environment you're in.

But he said nothing would change his mind in regards to that.

Nathan didn't want to tell the team as a whole, he wanted to get round and tell every player individually. We said we wouldn't do anything until the next day.

So that, one, he could sleep on his decision, and, two, perhaps Stephen could spend some time trying to convince him to go to the World Cup. It was just in case his decision was a bit reactionary or a bit rash. We weren't sure that it was, but we'd give him the time to reconsider.

The lads took him out that night, and the next morning he was still adamant that he was retiring, so we had to go to the next plan, which was the timing of it, the announcement, the mechanics of what we go through.

On Thursday we went out to The Cut, a golf course 100 km out of Perth, and had a great day there. The day off was what Flem was talking about when he said later, 'Look, we did everything we could. We took him out to dinner, shouted him a round of golf. We tried to change his mind, we've done our best, but nothing's changed his mind.'

John Bracewell: On that day [Thursday] I'd scheduled, months before, that we'd all have a complete day off, players and management. The guys had organised to play golf, and it so happened it was two hours out of town. The timing of that wasn't ideal, in that communication isn't easy when people are wandering around a golf course. It was a bit of a numbing sort of day.

When you get a breaking story, journalists want that story, and they get a bit shirty, perhaps at times even a little bit immature, about the amount of attention they think they deserve in regard to the story. They'd heard whispers, but it wasn't going to be announced until the next day.

Once the players were told, it was always going to get out. Players ring their wives, and New Zealand is too small a country to have secrets.

Stephen Fleming: We went out to dinner and I went through the process of asking, 'Is there anything I can do? What do you need?' I'm sure a lot of other people did too. But it was for my closure, not his. I didn't want to walk away having the feeling that I hadn't done anything to help him get through.

My respect for him was too high to try to treat him with presents at the door, to treat him in some special way to change his mind. It was more a case of, 'It's been a great run, let's move on'. I knew straight away that it was a genuine decision.

The players were immensely disappointed, and they also struggled for closure, to live with the fact that a player who was a senior figure in the side, who they all expected to be there until the World Cup at least, wasn't going to be there.

Next morning we held the press conference and I left that night for Christchurch.

January 26, 2007: Nathan Astle is
Retiring from International Cricket

NZPA: Lack of enjoyment and motivation are the major factors behind Nathan Astle's decision to retire from international cricket, he said today.

Astle rocked his New Zealand cricket team-mates in Perth, calling time on his glittering 12-season international career.

The veteran all-rounder said he came to the decision just two days before the match against England in Adelaide on Tuesday, having consulted close friends and family.

'Just the enjoyment and motivation (are missing), it's been something I've been fighting with for about the last eight months,' Astle said.

'At this level you've got to have that motivation and for me the enjoyment side is huge, and it's not there any more.'

Astle, 35, announced his retirement from international cricket at a press conference at the team's Perth hotel, seated alongside captain Stephen Fleming and coach John Bracewell. He only informed his team-mates after the Adelaide match, with Bracewell saying it came out of the blue.

It comes two days before the Black Caps were to play Australia here in the Tri-Series — and just six weeks before the start of the World Cup, which would have been Astle's fourth.

John Bracewell: You can be at a stage in your life when you reach a crossroad, where the enjoyment of how you were as a kid with some things is not the same as when you're a parent. Could you say it's a matter of growing up? Certainly, and perhaps you don't need to look any deeper than that for Nathan's motivation.

Once I'd walked out of that press conference in Perth, it felt like a ton of bricks had lifted off my shoulders. What I said at the conference wasn't hard to explain, because it was the truth. But conspiracy theories were still spun, as you'll see in this excerpt from the *New Zealand Herald*. That's one of the reasons why I've explained in detail in this chapter how the decision was reached, why the conference was in Perth, not Adelaide, and have also had Stephen and John explain what happened as they saw it.

January 27, 2007: Astle Decision Doesn't Add Up

Some of our more cynically-minded cricket followers — and I include myself in this category — might be having just a little difficulty digesting the reasons and explanations behind Nathan Astle's shock retirement decision.

The man who last year said he was ready to throw the game away if the selectors continued to play silly-buggers with his career could hardly have picked a stranger time or place to step down from cricket.

Nor could he have given a more puzzling explanation.

Here we are, halfway through what's supposed to be a high-powered Tri-Series in Australia, perched on one of the most isolated outreaches on the planet — a game against the world champions just a day away — and Astle would like us to accept that he's merely had a change of heart.

Perhaps if he had been in the middle of a purple patch with the bat or at the end of a series, it would be easier to swallow the assertion that he's woken up one morning and suddenly decided to walk.

But the facts are he's been struggling with the bat, threatened by the selectors and shuffled around the order by the coach, to the extent that his World Cup place was starting to look anything but secure.

On top of that, New Zealand's opening batting combination has reached a crisis point this season.

Add to the mix the resurgent form of former New Zealand opener Lou Vincent, who has been recalled on the back of some solid innings in the domestic State Shield competition, and it's clear the pressure was starting to build on Astle and the selectors.

So, what about the idea that coach John Bracewell and the management team have approached Astle, offering to assist him through a dignified retirement rather than announcing that he's been axed?

Astle also mentioned that he'd made the decision over the past week and was the 'only' one who realised, when he walked out to bat against England at Adelaide last Tuesday, that he was about to play his final international innings.

If that was the case, then why on earth would he continue on to Perth to announce his retirement? Why would he insist on carrying on to a distant city — the best part of an eight-and-a-half-hour flight from his home-town of Christchurch — to announce that he didn't want to play?

Richard Boock, *New Zealand Herald*

Coming back home was probably not as emotional as the days in Australia when I was wrestling with the decision. I wouldn't pretend it hadn't been an emotional time. But once I'd told my family and team-mates, it was easier to deal with it all.

About the only time it all came flooding back was when I was in my room in Perth and got a text message from Flem saying, 'Mate, you had a great career, thoroughly enjoyed it and I'll miss you'. That hit home.

Back in Christchurch, Kelly was a bit emotional, and my mum too, but I wasn't too upset. I think I'd dealt with a lot of those feelings in Australia.

I've had no second thoughts, which I thought I might have, especially when I sat and watched the team playing without me on television. But the thought that I'd done the wrong thing really didn't enter my head, which gives me peace of mind.

Watching for the first time was a little bit weird, seeing Lou

[Vincent] walk out with Flem and knowing it had been me just a few days before. But it wasn't something that made me feel sad or hollow or anything like that. I think it was that I'd been wrestling with retirement for so long that I'd been anticipating what it would be like.

Looking back, one thing that always sticks in my mind was when I was a young kid sitting in the office of the high-performance centre at Lincoln, waiting to see Dayle Hadlee, and John Howell [the director of coaching at that time], walked in. (It was just after we'd been to the West Indies, where I'd got back-to-back hundreds.)

He said, 'Congratulations Nathan, but I've got no idea how you did it'.

I replied, 'Why is that?'.

'Well, you haven't got the greatest technique, and it'll be interesting, once they work you out, how you'll go at international level.'

I now think that's quite funny, but it stuck in my mind all through the next decade. I wouldn't call it motivation exactly, but perhaps in some underlying way it was.

In general, I've been a lucky man with my career. I have no major regrets at all. I've had some bumps on the way, tried some things when I was struggling that I should have been strong enough to reject. But I was able to do it my way, and for most of those years, life was hugely enjoyable.

The Time is Near

Several months into retirement, the biggest surprise for me is that the little bit of doubt over whether I should have left international cricket has never nagged at me. I haven't started rethinking it, I haven't missed the life at all, and I haven't regretted my decision whatsoever.

With the World Cup in the West Indies being screened on television here, I had expected that I might get the odd pang about not being there with the team. But all I ever did in the early games was check the scores, just to see how the guys were going. I should mention that when I was playing, I was never one to sit and watch hours of cricket anyway. Just watching was something that never appealed to me.

With two little kids at home in the morning, getting up at 6.30, when the World Cup games were on, I wouldn't have had much choice anyway. All they wanted to watch was the Disney Playhouse channel, so cricket became secondary to that. If I got a chance, I'd flick over in the commercial breaks, but that was as far as it went.

I knew what the guys were going through, but I didn't have any feelings about wanting to be there with them.

For myself, life after international cricket has revolved around my family, catching up with lost time from when I was travelling. When my son, Liam, was going through the stages of learning to walk, and starting to get a real little personality, I missed out on a lot of that, because I was away playing cricket. That was sad for me, because he was my first child, and it would have been great to be around when that was happening.

Since I've retired, I've been there when Alyssa took her first steps, as she started to show her personality, and began to really interact with people. That's been great. I regret not seeing it with Liam, and I consider myself lucky to have been there so much with Alyssa throughout that stage. It's an amazing thing, above anything I've ever done in my life before. I've been a house-husband really, while Kelly does a part-time job in a pharmacy.

I've looked around at a few possibilities with businesses or jobs for myself, because I do want to get out and keep busy, but so far I haven't decided on anything.

Being home with the two children, especially at the age they are now, has been fantastic. While cricket has taken me away a lot, it's been good enough to me to allow the luxury of spending several months with my kids, rather than having to finish the game and go straight back into a job. I've certainly got a massive amount of respect for a mother bringing up children on her own, which at times was what Kelly had to do when I toured.

Once Kelly and I started seeing each other, it took us very little time to get more serious. From the time we first went out to when we were engaged was a year, and a year after that we were married. In an odd twist, her younger sister Cherie ended up marrying my old school and cricketing mate Craig McMillan. Our kids are pretty much the same age too. Call me old-fashioned, but before I proposed, I asked Kelly's father, Kevin Winter, for her hand in marriage. That almost went pear-shaped. Her parents were at our place one night, and Kevin loves his golf. I said to him, 'Mate, come out to the garage for a minute, I've got this new club for you to have a look at'.

At that stage, we were in a little townhouse with the garage attached. So I took him out there, and I said to him, 'Aw mate, I haven't got a golf club at all. I wanted to ask if I could have your daughter's hand in marriage.'

At the top of his lungs, he shouted, 'YOU WHAT?'.

So I had a little pause, and then asked, 'Is that a confirmation or not?'. I was also worried that they'd hear us inside. He said it had taken him by surprise, but he was more than happy, shook my hand and said, 'That'd be great'.

I took Kelly out for dinner a few days later. At that stage David Howman was my manager, the lawyer who is now in Montreal with the World Anti-Doping Agency. David then lived in Wellington. After dinner I said to Kelly that David was in town, and it'd be nice if we went to David's hotel to catch up.

We went into the Millennium, in Cathedral Square, and went up to the room. Initially, Kelly didn't even click that it was a little weird that I already had a key to David's room. We walked in and there was a big bunch of roses and a bottle of champagne that I'd arranged. I got down on one knee and asked her to marry me.

I'd also organised for her mum and dad, and my parents, to come in. About half an hour later there was a knock at the door, and I said it'd just be room service. I opened the door, and it was Kelly's parents.

kelly: I must say Nathan did a terrific job with his proposal. I didn't suspect a thing when we went to the hotel.

We were married on 8 April 2000, in the chapel at St Michael's school, where Kelly went to school. That winter the New Zealand team wasn't touring, so about two weeks after we were married we headed off to an English summer and I played league cricket for Accrington. We were able to make some quick visits to Europe, and enjoyed our time together in England.

> *kelly*: When the New Zealand team went to England in 2004 Liam was just a baby. We travelled to be with Nathan. Liam kept waking every four hours, and in a hotel room there was nowhere to go to get any sleep when he woke.

Even though it was great to have our first child there, it was hard. You're so happy they're there, but I look at some photos and my eyes are hanging out of my head. I didn't realise how tired I was at the time, but looking back, I was physically exhausted.

New Zealand Cricket has changed its attitude towards wives and partners going on tour. There was a stage where partners were welcome only on certain dates. That was pretty hard, because if your partner was working it wasn't always possible to get time off at those particular times. But for some years now they've been pretty flexible.

Now that every player has their own room, partners can turn up and not put anyone out. I think it has to be that way now. You're away so much and for so long, and guys are in relationships and are parents. If you're happy at home, you're going to play better for the team.

> *kelly*: Since then, when Nathan's been away and the kids and I haven't travelled with him, I've had so much support from my sister Cherie. At times I don't know what I would have done without her. We spend so much time together,

and we've had kids at about the same time, and because she's married to a cricketer too we totally understand how each other is feeling when the team is touring.

Cherie and I have spent a lot of time at each other's places, even stayed overnight, which is great company for us — adult company.

I think I thought it'd get easier, but in fact it got harder to cope when Nathan was gone. I did quite a bit of travelling with Nathan when we didn't have children, but it's too hard with children. We learned that in England.

There's no easy answer to it. I was one who always wanted to see my kids. In my later years it got harder and harder, with Liam coming along, and then Alyssa, I was always aware that I was missing that growing-up period.

When I was away touring I could go out to golf, go to the pub, go shopping, do whatever I wanted to. But Kelly was stuck at home, and that annoyed her a bit. For your sanity you've got to get some time to yourself. You love your kids to bits, but you do need a break sometimes, and you need some adult contact. Over time, I got a lot better about understanding what Kel was going through. In the early stages, if I went out just for a quiet drink on tour, I couldn't understand why Kelly wasn't that interested in talking about it on the phone.

I didn't fully realise how hard it was for Kel until I finished my international career. I only have the kids a couple of days a week, while she's at work. I've loved it, but it's pretty full on, and to do it 24/7 by yourself is a huge job. I have a lot more respect for what parents on their own are coping with now.

There were times when I did feel guilty about it when I was on tour, but I couldn't just stay in my hotel room eating room service food, because that does your head in. When you see a cricketer travelling the world and staying in fancy hotels, it's easy to forget that often we have families at home and we miss them just as much as anyone else misses their kids. It can be very tough.

As far as the cricket side went, I tended to try to leave it at the ground. Sure, if there was something I was really not happy about I'd discuss it with Kelly, but by and large I left it there.

kelly: Nathan's never brought it home. I couldn't tell from how he walks in the door how it's gone in the game.

Kelly loves her cricket, but she's not a fanatic about the game. To me, that's a good thing. I couldn't think of anything worse than walking through the door, having a bad day, and my wife saying, 'I don't think you did this right, and you should work on this, and change that'.

The fact that she doesn't analyse the game in any way helped separate any feelings from the game from what was happening at home. The kids made it even easier. When I walked through the door they'd greet me with a big smile, and whatever I'd been worrying about would tend to fade away: I'd think, 'Hey, it's only a game of cricket'. The kids put it all in perspective.

kelly: I have friends that go back to school days, and then, with the cricket partners, we have a coffee group in Christchurch, that we've organised ourselves. When he's batting, I watch on television, but I don't sit there and watch the whole game. I enjoyed the whole atmosphere of going to the ground, but it's harder with kids.

Over the years, Kelly and I have played a few sports against each other. I feel pretty confident about table tennis, darts and backyard cricket. But I won't take her on at swimming. I always reckon that

I could beat her, but I prefer not to race her to make sure.

kelly: I swam at national age group championships. I started at a really young age, at New Brighton, training morning and night. I never won a title at age group nationals, but I made finals and won place medals.

In the end, I found it hard to balance schoolwork and swimming, and to be honest I ended up almost hating it, because I had no life outside the swimming. We started at a young age, but it wasn't a case of being pushed into it by Mum and Dad. I was the one who wanted to do it for a start, but eventually I think I just burned out. For quite a long time I didn't even want to go near a pool.

With the kids, I've gone back a bit. I quite enjoy getting in the pool with Nathan, because I think it's one sport I could beat him at.

After I left school I worked as a nurse aide, and then in a hospital pharmacy, where I trained to be a dispensary technician.

I worked in the office for Kiwi Air while it lasted, and have worked in pharmacies for the last nine years. I didn't think I'd miss the work when the children arrived, but I did, so now I work a couple of days a week.

Nathan and I agree that the kids have quite similar personalities. They've both got stubborn streaks in them, which comes through from both of us. Alyssa's a bit more mischievous than Liam, which is very much Nathan.

They both seem to be well co-ordinated. Alyssa takes every opportunity to pick up a golf club and hit the ball, which she could do quite well, even before she was a year old.

I haven't pushed Liam towards cricket at all, but if he wants to pick up a cricket bat, he knows how to stand and how to hit the ball. He can swing a golf club too.

For my own sport now, I've always said that I'd like to play one or two seasons for Canterbury, and I'm sure if they wanted me I'd enjoy it enormously, because I'd only be playing for the team on the day. There wouldn't be any of the pressures of form that come when you're working to be in the Black Caps as well. At this stage, Canterbury has a very young team, and I'd hope that one or two of the younger guys might pick up a wee thing or two from me while I was there. Canterbury's been very good to me over a long period of time. It wouldn't be a feeling of obligation to them, just something I've thought for a while that I'd like to do. The other thing that would be huge for me, with our young family, is that you're only away for four or five days, and the whole season is over inside five months.

Initially, I'll be looking for work outside the game. What I would like to do is some coaching on a one-to-one basis. I couldn't see myself coaching a team. To be absolutely blunt about it, even as a player I struggle to sit and watch a whole day of cricket. It'd be interesting for me to find out what sort of one-on-one coach I would make. There's a tendency with some coaches to almost clone players, whereas I believe you still need to have some individuality. You can tweak some of the finer points, but you don't make a full overhaul of what they're doing. If you tell someone to change what he knows, what's worked for him, a lot of the time it'll be for the worse.

I might change my mind, but right now to do some specialist coaching with young Canterbury players is what I'd hope to do. Not straight away, but perhaps in a few years.

I am pretty optimistic for the immediate future for the Black Caps. My only real worry is the fitness of Shane Bond. He's such a crucial part of the team, and round the traps I haven't seen a man of his calibre ready to step in and take over if he is injured or decides to give the game away.

We have a lot of young talent coming through on the batting side. Guys like Flem will still be around, Macca's playing well again, and I'm sure Hamish Marshall will also find form once more. There's also Lou Vincent, Matthew Sinclair and Ross Taylor, who is still a young kid, but very talented. So I think the batting is pretty much covered, especially given the quality of Jacob Oram, Brendon McCullum and Dan Vettori. The only big sticking point would be that if we lost Shane Bond it would be difficult to find someone to spearhead the attack the way he has over the last few years.

When the Black Caps reached the semi-finals of the World Cup, I enjoyed a new experience. The National Bank asked me to go to Auckland, where Kyle Mills and I hosted a breakfast to watch New Zealand play Sri Lanka. We started at 4 a.m., so we missed some of the start, but from four o'clock on I watched the game to its conclusion. I found it very interesting: sitting at the back of a room, watching with a mainly male audience, seeing how people watch a game of cricket. For me, that was something brand new. I'd watched cricket on television with my family, maybe with guys in the team, but I'd never sat with a big group of guys watching a game of cricket.

There were a couple of comments made when we were losing, and you could almost see people pull themselves up because they knew Kyle and I were in the room. Of the three other teams in the semi-finals, Sri Lanka was the team that made me the most nervous. I would have honestly preferred us to play Australia or South Africa. Sri Lanka is just a dangerous side (and, in passing, I thought they would have put up more of a fight in the final against Australia).

Watching our semi-final against Sri Lanka, I thought Malinga bowled outstandingly well, and the way Jayawardene constructed his innings of 115 was brilliant. He batted out of his skin. They were two match-winning performances, and, sadly, we couldn't match them on the day. Jayawardene led them to such a good total that it was one of those days where the game was pretty much taken away from us.

Surprisingly, I then found that even though I'm out of it, some of the bitter criticism the team copped from people in the media still hurt. Of course, many people were disappointed with the loss, but all New Zealanders should know that every guy in that team, from the captain right through to the management team, would have been hurting 10 times more than anyone else in the country. I know that they went there with high hopes, and I had high hopes too. I honestly believed they would win it. Some critics don't understand how, after a match like that, sitting in the shed, it would have been dead quiet for a long time. Guys would have been sitting there, wondering what they could have done differently, reflecting on what could have been.

Before the tournament we were ranked third in the world, and we finished third, so we played to our ranking — yet the team was hammered for it. I know that people in New Zealand want the team to win — and the guys in the team would dearly love to do that for them — but to me a lot of guys in the media are very up and down. They run red-hot when we're winning and then have a huge crack at the team when we don't win. It'd be nice to see a more reasoned approach.

Realising that the guys on the pitch are giving it their all would be a good start. Players don't go out there to drop catches. They don't go out to get nought or bowl wides. Sometimes, in the game of cricket, no matter how hard you try, things just go wrong.

Statistics

Batting and fielding averages

	Mat	Inns	NO	Runs	HS	Ave	SR	100	50	Ct
Tests	81	137	10	4702	222	37.02		11	24	70
First-class	171	272	24	9321	223	37.58		19	50	134
ODIs	223	217	14	7090	145*	34.92	72.64	16	41	83
Twenty20 Int.	4	4	1	74	40*	24.66	110.44	0	0	3

Bowling averages

	Mat	Balls	Runs	Wkts	BBI	Ave	Econ	5	10
Tests	81	5688	2143	51	3/27	42.01	2.26	0	0
First-class	171	13441	4897	150	6/22	32.64	2.18	2	0
ODIs	223	4850	3809	99	4/43	38.47	4.71	0	0
Twenty20 Int.	4	41	50	4	3/20	12.50	7.31	0	0